WHY WAIT FOR EULOGIES

Joyful expressions on gratitude, life, and legacy with a circle of friends

LAKSHMI SUNDAR

To all those who made me who I am

CONTENTS

PART I
THE UNIMAGINED ARRIVAL IN THE UNITED STATES

It was a chilly, super windy, Memorial Day weekend when my mother, brother, and I landed at JFK Airport in New York City. It was my mother's fortieth birthday. My father had moved to the United States earlier in the year for a job and we were following him several months later. As I stepped off the plane, I was overwhelmed with emotions. Besides having been very sick on the journey, the situation itself felt absolutely absurd. If someone had told me a year ago that I would be moving from India to the United States, I would have thought they had lost their mind. Growing up in a middle-class family in India with little money to spare and no relatives overseas meant that I could go abroad by one of three means - by getting a job in the hospitality sector to travel for free, by saving a lot of money, or by marrying someone who lived in a foreign land. After watching a leading Indian movie star couple romance in Disney Land and Niagara Falls on screen, I decided that I would latch on to one of the first two options and take at least one coveted trip to the United States.

But as they say, life is what happens when you are busy making plans. One October evening, on a plane ride home from a business trip, my father spotted a job opening at the World Bank. Never one to shy away from taking chances, he spent a few rupees on postage and mailed over his resume. In a rapid unfolding of events, which felt more like fiction than real life, he was offered a job, and at the age of fifty, when many men in India began counting down the years to retirement, he decided that he was going to give his kids the security of an American education and life.

And just like that, the somewhat awkward, kind of smart and curious, sort of well-spoken multilingual me, who had lots of insecurities about her looks and lack of wealth/social standing had arrived in the coveted land.

There are so many immigrant narratives out there, each with their share of pain, struggle, separation, loss, excitement, triumph, and euphoria. I experienced each of these emotions in abundance. But each time I think back on my journey, there is another feeling that floods my heart, one of deep gratitude. Many immigrants may feel appreciative for a multitude of things in their new homeland. But to me, my evolution and growth on both the personal and professional fronts would not have been possible without a village of humans who helped me along the way.

This book features tributes that I penned to ten beautiful souls who I met on this journey; women who are older and younger than me; women who were classmates, colleagues, bosses, and fellow moms with young kids; women seemed to be put on my path exactly when I needed them most. I would be remiss if I did not clarify that there were many men who helped me significantly on this journey as well. But the bonds I formed with these women were deep, and to this day, I count on each of them for their friendship, love, support, and guidance.

I debated on the best way to express my gratitude in a meaningful manner and realized that life does not present many formal occasions to give thanks. Performance reviews, birthdays, weddings, and anniversaries are a few of the milestones where thoughtful recognition is given. The closest approximation of delivering very deeply felt tributes appears to be tied to death. Speeches at funerals and memorial services, obituaries, and words of remembrances all acknowledge and celebrate the impact of those around us. Yet, the saddest part of these well-intended, beautifully articulated tributes, is that the person who is being recognized does not get to hear or read a single word.

I did not want to wait. I wanted my friends to know now what they mean to me, the impact they have had on my journey, and how much I cherish their presence. Coincidentally, the idea of putting my gratitude in writing came to me as a result of thinking about death. I was exchanging routine check-in texts with my friend, Suzanne, who is at the stage of cancer where she laughingly says she has lived past her expiration date. I started writing a letter of gratitude to her and the rest simply followed.

Every moment I spent writing was time I eagerly looked forward to with each passing hour recording more smiles on my face. But that was just the beginning of this joy ride. Before I knew it, I was surrounded by my friends' emotional reactions, which floored me. Then, to understand how they came to be these special people, we traveled back in time to their childhood spaces, experiences, and emotions, trips that spilled forth joy, laughter, and tears. Through these conversations, I began to understand how my friends grew up a world away from me; I got a peek into their dreams and insecurities; I heard about the foods they ate and the advice they would give to their younger selves; And last but not least, as we talked about reflections and legacy, we came full circle; we finished a process that started with tributes and ended with more love and appreciation infused into our friendships.

As a bonus, each of my friends left me a little gift of food. Not too long ago, angered by the divisive headlines, I set about applying to and getting selected to give a TEDx talk on how food is the ultimate, speechless language that brings people together. As a foodie, I couldn't be more delighted that each friend gave me a gift of their favorite recipe. Each time I create one of their favorite meals in my kitchen, a part of their life becomes intertwined with mine.

My hope in sharing my experiences is that it will spur more people to give thanks to the people who matter. As you read about my journey and my friends, it may remind you of your journey and the friends and loved ones that enabled you along the way. I'd love for you to pause for a second and relive and feel those moments. And if it makes you want to reach out to your loved ones and share a cup of coffee, a meal, a phone call, or an impromptu visit, that's one more way you have recognized the importance of these individuals in your life, shown to them that they matter, that you care, while they are here to feel the joy. In the process, just like me, you may experience the multiplicative power of gratitude, where a little expression spills forth joy many times over.

PART II
THE NEW TO THE UNITED STATES ME

What was my identity when I landed in the United States? Who was I as a person and what did I look like? Did I even speak English and what were my values? Did I wear Indian clothes and eat curry? These questions followed me for many years after my arrival.

The teen who stepped off that plane and into a new land was a wannabe in so many ways. I wanted to see the world, to learn, to have the means to buy more than two sets of clothes a year, to be more sophisticated like my wealthier friends, to cook and bake without worrying about food bills, to feel more beautiful than my imperfect self, and to go back to India someday and show people that I had come a long way from the average looking, acned, middle class, unsophisticated, bullied kid who never quite fit in. Yes, now that I think about it, I carried a lot of baggage along with my hopes and dreams. And why did I not mention falling in love and finding a partner? That's because when I was in school, I met this guy who was assigned as my lab partner in Chemistry and before I left India, a chemistry of a different sort had developed. We committed to staying in touch and planned to finish our higher education, land good jobs, and then find our way back to each other.

So, how did this aspirant me come into being? I was born to middle-class parents who grew up a decade apart a few streets from one another in the southern Indian city of Thiruvanantha-puram. Dad fought with his parents, who wanted him to be a schoolteacher, and went on to study engineering in Chennai, and then left for the United States to study and work before returning to India. Mom grew up sheltered as the first daughter after four sons and when she was still a teenager, was set up to be married off to a "foreign returned eligible bachelor". Before she had said a single word to my father, she was his wife, leaving her secure upbringing to move 1,500 miles to Rourkela, in northeast India, where she knew no one and did not speak the local language.

I was the firstborn grandchild in both families, a bit of an initial disappointment for my paternal grandmother because I was not the "prodigal" son. From an early age, I was disciplined about school and grew up with two broad messages. Mom's mantra was, "you need to learn everything to be a good woman, a wife, and a mother, because family is everything"; Dad's advice was, "there is no difference whether you are a daughter or a son. Just study well, get financially independent, and then find a spouse to continue the journey". So, those two philosophies permeated my growing up years.

Dad worked, and mom stayed home to raise us. Dad was driven and ambitious, and when he did not get what he wanted at work, he quit, moved on to a new company, and the family followed.

. . .

Thus, my childhood involved frequent moves, which came with the forming and breaking of friendships. Given India is a fairly diverse country, each place we moved to had its language and social norms and I was always the outsider trying to fit in. Besides being a transplant in areas that my family was not from, being an outsider took on many forms. In a community where girls were expected to be docile and soft-spoken, I was quite outspoken and had a temper. In a country where fair skin and perfect features defined beauty, I was darker skinned, had big teeth, and did not fit any compartment of traditionally defined beauty standards. In a group of wealthy classmates, I was the one with two sets of clothes who did not own any makeup or go to a salon. Among friends who jetted off to exotic locales on their summer vacations, I was the outlier staying with my grandparents in a small town in southern India. As girls learned to cook traditional meals, I was more fascinated with baking and exotic ingredients. As my friends planned for comfortable existences at home post marriage, I dreamed of studying hotel management and getting a job to travel overseas. This list could be several pages in length, but you get the gist of it. The young woman who left her country for the first time wanted to be many things she was not.

And it was this dreamer who stepped off the plane on that cold, summer day, unaware that someday, she would get everything her heart desired and would frequently refer to herself as the chosen one for the fantastic life she was gifted.

And now, to answer the questions that I posed at the beginning of this section - like many Indians, my entire schooling was done in English and I spoke the language beautifully. My father pushed me to participate in elocutions and debates, something that led me to be quite a fearless speaker. In India, I wore Indian clothes, and I swore to myself that moving to a foreign land would not take away my Indianness.

The first few months in the US were like heaven on earth - joyous and carefree. Dad had a great job. For the first time, mom and I did not go grocery shopping worrying about prices and the money we had on hand. In India, my mom and I stood in line at the store with our ration card, waiting to pick up rice, oil, and other necessities at government-regulated prices. In contrast, here, we walked out of Giant (our local grocery store) with tubs of ice cream, packets of donuts, and big bags of potato chips. It was a glorious summer with nothing to do, so I lounged around and got hooked on "Days of our Lives", an American soap opera. We went sightseeing like true tourists. Thanks to our neighbors, we tried pizza, pasta, and more. And since I was scheduled to start school in the Fall, I got an opportunity to buy all kinds of good clothes. It was all super exciting and amazing - a journey in a new land, an opportunity to experience a freer life, a portal into becoming the new me. It was this young woman who set foot on campus that Fall, looking for acceptance and growth in her new home.

PART III

THERE ARE PARTS OF WHO I AM THAT I OWE TO EACH OF YOU

MARCIA

S tate of mind: Nervous and lost at school and life

After all the fun and relaxation over the summer, reality arrived in the Fall. School was about to begin and I was nervous and lost. Being a new immigrant, my father had limited money and yet had written a big check out for my tuition. I wanted to do well but was clueless about whether I would or not. I knew chemistry, but nothing about business, and here I was about to embark on graduate studies when most people my age were finishing their sophomore year of college.

I must have looked like a lost soul on campus during those early days. An outsider, yet again; a solitary figure, devoid of friends, clutching on to her map and trying to navigate her way around campus. I was afraid to ask for directions, wanting to appear confident. I thought people were staring at me because I looked different. I scanned faces, feeling overwhelmed, unsure, and scared, praying that someone would tap my shoulder and offer to help.

MY FIRST AMERICAN FRIEND

I was gazing at the unfamiliar faces in the campus bookstore when I dropped the books I was carrying. Out of the crowds came a petite, friendly woman, her smile radiating to her eyes, asking me if I needed help. I was on the verge of tears, but she helped me pick up my books and introduced herself, "Hi, I'm Marcia, and aren't we in the same accounting class?" With that introduction, I had found my **FIRST** American friend.

After that initial exchange of pleasantries, Marcia, a super friendly person, always acknowledged me and introduced me to others. I did not know anything about how this new place worked, what people thought, and, of course, how I should behave. Marcia, on the other hand, was comfortable in her skin, talking seamlessly with people, networking with professors, and managing her classes and school work with ease. I don't remember all of our classes together but do recollect teaming up with Marcia, Rob, and Gianni on a market research project investigating the potential of solar panels. Marcia probably did not realize how much I learned by watching her as she talked to the business we were assisting, expressed her thoughts at group discussions, and wrote up summaries for our assignments. I also found comfort in having her as part of my team, especially as I navigated unfamiliar terrain; getting together late evenings for group discussions and being in the company of male friends in their apartments without any parental presence.

Besides helping me with my school journey, Marcia was part of many firsts I experienced in the US. Marcia was the first American friend who came to our home. She was curious to learn about us and our customs and chatted away comfortably with my mother in English and my grandma through signs and actions. I had my first dinner at an American's home when she asked me to join her and her husband for Easter. I painted Easter eggs, learned about the Quaker faith, and was surprised to learn that Americans could be vegetarian too. Marcia was the first person to vouch for me professionally. She landed a job before me and when I coincidentally interviewed at a different arm of the same company, she voluntarily jumped right in with a reference. I was introduced to the phrase "over the hill" when I attended her 30th birthday celebrations with this theme. In addition to all the socializing and fun, Marcia and her husband showed me first-hand the power of activism, both being passionate advocates for causes they strongly believed in. I tagged along with Marcia on her volunteering excursions to mentor inner-city girls in the historically underserved neighborhoods of Washington DC. This is where I encountered poverty in America first hand, a condition that I had seen aplenty in India.

As our friendship grew, I shared Marcia's excitement around her pregnancy, her sadness around her miscarriage, the birth of her kids, the trials and tribulations of their growing up years, her various career moves, her transition from the hectic suburbs of Washington DC to the idyllic relaxed pace of life in Maine, her increasing activism to make a difference, the loss of her beloved mom, and, of course, her evolution and growth as a woman, mom, wife, and professional. She, in turn, celebrated the arrival of my kids, provided counsel on their tough growing up stages, shared perspectives on our ever-changing needs as women and, of course, joyously exchanged globetrotting tales.

Unlike our early years, Marcia and I are now separated by hundreds of miles, a distance we attempt to bridge through infrequent phone calls and emails, always picking up right where we left off. I don't know if Marcia keeps copious notes of our chats or has a brilliant memory, but with every catch-up, she makes sure to remember and follow up on all the relevant topics from the previous discussion.

There are so many things I have learned from Marcia over the years; so many ways in which she has inspired me. But most of all, I am so grateful that she took this lost, confused, sad, newly arrived immigrant, held her hand, and supported her through one of the toughest transitions of her life.

A Q&A with Marcia

What was your reaction to the tribute?

My dear friend Marcia, who lives with her husband in picturesque Maine in their environmentally friendly home, was very surprised and grateful when she read the tribute to her.

"It was terribly kind of you to do this, Lakshmi, and it speaks as much about you and your generous spirit as it does about me. You are a keen observer of the world around you and are curious and open to new things and experiences. You manage to stay positive through life's ups and downs and your ability to maintain friendships over time is amazing."

Marcia's response brought a big smile to my face.

What was your favorite memory of our time together?

I asked Marcia if any of her memorable moments of our interactions matched mine. Marcia recalled two separate incidents, both of which I had forgotten until now.

"You invited me over to your apartment one day after class and I was quite excited because I love Indian food. Indeed, it was delicious. However, it was spiced so hot, I had tears running down my cheeks. You felt bad about this, I could tell...

The next time you invited me over to eat, you told me that you'd solved the food problem. That sounded great. To my slight disappointment though, it was spaghetti, not Indian food. However, I shortly discovered the spaghetti was equally hot and, again, tears ran down my cheeks and my ears turned bright red. Turns out, you'd used a lot of chilies, same as before! You apparently thought it was the Indian food itself that had caused the problem and not the chilies seasoning. I thought that was funny."

I was now curious to know more about her. How did she grow up? What did her family look like? Did she have any insecurities like me? What did she want to be when she grew up? As a foodie, I was curious to also know what meal times looked like in her home. I rattled off my questions and learned that a world away, my friend and I grew up sharing a few similarities.

. . .

How and where did you grow up?

Marcia was the oldest of three girls born to a physician father and a stay at home mom. Just like me, she moved around a lot as a kid.

"As a small child, my family moved several times. When I was 9, though, we moved to Madison, Wisconsin, where I lived from 4th grade through high school.

Madison was a pretty wholesome place to grow up, with access to parks, fields, and lakes. Our neighborhood, a subdivision with about 40 houses, was somewhat set off from the rest of the city so, during the day, my two sisters and I were free to go out and run around. We liked to play croquet, pretend we owned horses, ride our bikes, explore along the railroad tracks, and pick flowers in a nearby meadow. It was a much freer time for children than what we see today."

What was your personality like as a child?

As the oldest kid, Marcia says that she was probably a little "bossy". But this bossy kid learned to be an advocate at a young age from her mom.

"We were schooled by our Mother to be kind to one another and other people. There was a growing awareness in grade school of the discrimination faced by African Americans. Although our school was not diverse, we listened to a radio program called The Darker Brother, about racial harmony, and I remember thinking, "Why can't we all just get along?" I was idealistic that way."

Marcia's childhood anecdotes led me to incorrectly believe that she had always been super confident.

"You described me as "totally comfortable in her skin". Most people, myself included, have some degree of self-doubt... and I think that's healthy."

What did you want to be when you grew up?

Yet another hallmark of childhood memories is just thinking about what you want to be when you grow up. I have to say that I was really bummed to learn that Marcia did not end up becoming what she thought she wanted to be, since I would have absolutely voted for her.

"For many years, it was President of the United States so I could fix all the problems. Later it evolved into wanting to be a U.S. Senator."

While Marcia did not end up in high-profile political roles, she created an impact in each of the many roles that she pursued and to this day, in her semi-retired state, is active in giving back.

What did mealtimes look like when you were growing up? Any favorite food memories?

To me, no memories of childhood are complete without talking about food and mealtimes. To Marcia, food is synonymous with family, friends, and building bridges. She reminisced fondly about her childhood meals.

"At dinner time, Mom would ring an old school bell and we would come back from playing. The meal usually contained meat (or casserole with meat), a canned vegetable, and a starch (such as potatoes or rice). There was always a plate of sliced bread on the table if anyone was still hungry. My mother believed in serving a variety of foods, so the main

dishes ranged from chicken a la king, to liver, to meatloaf, to lasagna, to fried smelts, to cow's tongue, and tuna noodle casserole.

We always ate as a family in the dining room. My father, who was a doctor, liked to talk about serious subjects and did not appreciate kids being silly at the dinner table. So, if either of my sisters and I got rambunctious, we were sent to eat at the "baby table" in the kitchen. Since we were usually sent there one at a time, it was like being exiled."

I couldn't help but chuckle as I imagined Marcia being exiled from anything! If the daily meals involved discipline, her Christmas eve celebrations were anything but that. In fact, the family get-togethers around the holidays were all about togetherness.

"Christmas Eve was always a very special time in our household. My two grandmothers would be with us and, more often than not, my only aunt and uncle and their 3 children would join us. All the women would help put the meal together, including my sisters and me.

The meal usually consisted of ham or lamb, mashed potatoes, green beans, and a squash casserole. The crowning glory was the dessert, a Yule Log, made of delicious chocolate wafers and whipped cream to look like a wood log with candles on top. We would turn off all the lights and my mother would triumphantly parade in with the Yule Log. As the candles burned on it, the family would sing "Deck the Halls with bows of Holly" and "See the blazing Yule before us".

The tradition of the meal, the togetherness of our family, and the extreme deliciousness of the Yule Log dessert itself made it all very special."

Can you share a favorite recipe of yours with me?

I asked Marcia if she would make the foodie in me happy by sharing her favorite vegetarian recipe. Marcia shared her favorite tofu dish from Jeanne Lemlin's cookbook called, "Main Course Vegetarian Pleasures." This is a dish that even her picky eater husband loves. As someone who has yet to master the art of a well-prepared tofu dish, this one will make a frequent appearance along with Marcia anecdotes in my kitchen. (I have included this and all the other recipe gifts from my friends at the end of this book.)

What advice would you give to your younger self?

As I reminisced with Marcia about her childhood, I asked her if there was any advice she would give to her younger self.

> *"Life is unpredictable and what you set out to do will change a lot along the way. If you are open to new opportunities and challenges, life will probably work out."*

What do you want your legacy in the world to be?

I began this journey with Marcia with a tribute to her. I closed our conversation by asking her what she wanted her legacy in the world to be.

> *"I would like people to remember me as having made a difference in promoting a cleaner world and for doing so with kindness, creativity, and humor."*

She feels that she has been able to make a difference later in life through initiatives outside her career.

> *"After I stepped back from the workplace, I had the time to organize a group that succeeded in pushing for some really important*

environmental changes in Maine. That work, in turn, led to service on the board of Maine's premier environmental advocacy organization—a group that has helped Maine become a leader in addressing climate change, preserving water quality, promoting sustainable communities, and protecting wildlife and natural areas."

SECTION 2
SUE

State of mind: **Anxious about finding a good job and staying on in the US**

I had slowly eased into my new life in the United States. Thanks to a few new friends and acquaintances, I did not feel like a complete foreigner anymore. But the fairy tale landing soon encountered rough waters. Two years into life in the United States, my father was on the verge of losing his job. While a job loss in most instances leads to a loss of financial and emotional security, here, we also faced the prospect of being forced to return to India. My brother was in school and as the eldest child, I felt tremendous pressure to find a job that would at the very minimum enable us to stay on and for me to support his education.

Not only would I need a company to pick me over hundreds of other qualified candidates, but they would also have to sponsor me for a visa. I was convinced the odds were stacked against me. My friends had good work experiences, even before graduate school. They knew how to dress, to talk confidently, and inter-view well. Why would anyone want to hire me?

INDEBTED FOR THE WINGS
THAT HELPED ME FLY

INDEBTED – This is THE perfect word to describe how I feel about Sue, the woman who gave me, a young immigrant and a new graduate, the professional training, personal mentoring, and the ultimate set of wings I needed to soar to success.

I was a newly minted graduate, unsure of which area of Marketing I wanted to get into when one of my professors informed me about a position at Verizon. He was unsure whether my non-American demeanor and personality (my shyness with self-promotion, comfort level with hanging around in Indian clothes on campus, slight awkwardness in group settings, ...) would land me this job, but thought I might want to give it a try, nonetheless. As I set foot in my first set of corporate offices, dressed in a navy suit, adjusting my stockings and the bow on my blouse for the millionth time, I kept hearing the word "imposter". When I set eyes on the most immaculately groomed Sue, I lost all semblance of confidence. A team of researchers interviewed me and when Sue was done with her portion, she handed me a piece of paper with some data on it. She walked away, giving me some time to review the information and come up with a synopsis of what I had learned. I don't know what I said or did, but when I ended up landing the job, I experienced euphoria and disbelief for months on end.

Sue would later tell me that I apparently told her a story about deviled eggs during my interview. I did not even know what deviled eggs were at that stage, but it turns out that every time I said "develop", my accent made it sound like I was saying devilled! Sue took me under her wing and trained me on qualitative and quantitative research, how to write research reports, how to speak with clients, how to present in interesting ways, how to work with vendors, and so much more. As I was learning and growing into what Sue called a "talented researcher", the naïve young woman from India was also picking up lessons on fashion, pop culture, food, celebrations, and so much more.

Fashion: Sue introduced me to the world of designer clothes, shoes, bags, and more, and taught me the ropes to snag deals. At the time, several of the stores that sold designer brands for less had communal dressing rooms, and the first time Sue took me to one and wanted an opinion on an outfit, I was so overcome by shyness that I did not know in which direction to turn while people changed with no inhibitions. To this day, at key moments, I think about how Sue would react to a particular outfit.

Pop Culture: It was in Sue's car that I learned that a single sentence in the English language could be peppered with so many colorful words. Since I didn't own a car, Sue would often give me rides and it was on one such ride that I was introduced to Howard Stern. I think my body convulsed in shock at the barrage of words flowing through the airwaves and my head turned to the window trying to figure out how to face Sue.

Food: Sue is an amazing cook and baker. I was blown away by her surprise homemade brownies for my birthday, left salivating after trying her carrot cake, and inspired by the immaculate archives of Gourmet and Bon Appetit magazines that lined her home. We had dinner dates, where we devoured entire pies of Armand's deep-dish pizza and spent an evening grating fresh coconut the Indian way for the perfect Passover macaroons. Her talents no doubt influenced me to explore a more varied kaleidoscope of foods.

Fun: Sue made sure we worked hard but also had our share of fun. Staff meetings would be held at outlet malls where intense work discussions fueled by good coffee would be followed by an afternoon of shopping. When I became a manager for the first time, I wanted to be like Sue − a mentor who respected talent and also had fun.

Celebrations: Sue's middle name might as well be "giver". Birthday celebrations, bridal showers, baby showers − her colleagues were the recipients of her generous, perfectly curated celebrations. For the birth of my first child, she threw a shower that featured an elaborate coffee drink menu, with a barista on site!

For close to eight years, I was fortunate to have this woman mentor and coach me each day. She helped sponsor me for my green card and gain a permanent foothold in this country at a time when I needed it so badly (Thankfully, the situation with my dad changed as well, and we all were able to stay together). During this time, we also traveled from boss-employee to really good friends. A journey that saw her contemplating traveling to India for my wedding, debating on the perfect car to buy for a milestone birthday, agonizing over finding the right partner with whom she could have the much longed-for kid, showing up to celebrate my initiation into motherhood, celebrating the arrival of my second child, sharing her disappointment at not being recognized for her stellar work/sincerity, her getting married and welcoming the most special person in her life – her son Joey, and throwing the biggest party for his Bar Mitzvah.

Sue is not an easy person to reach; she barely calls or remembers to call back. We meet up only once every few years. But just recently, when I was back in the DC area, a quick meet up for a late lunch turned into a six-hour catch-up; the woman who gave me the wings to fly showing me yet again why she has become one of the most precious, inseparable parts of my life.

A Q&A with Sue

What was your reaction to the tribute?

Sue, a market researcher and a super-duper mom who lives in the suburbs of Washington DC with her son Joe admitted to getting very emotional at this tribute.

> *"Honestly, I was very emotional and flabbergasted reading this. The gestalt of this surprised and overwhelmed me and brought me to tears. It is not too often that someone takes the time to think about the impact you*

have had on their life and pays a tribute. Seeing this on paper moved me. I'd like to believe that this is the person I am and have been all my life; work and life have a strange way of imposing self-doubt on your capabilities."

Sue's reaction moved me to tears. I was surprised that she had not heard how special she was more often.

What was your favorite memory of our time together?

When I asked Sue if my favorite memories of our time together were the ones she recalled, she said I missed a pretty important one, where I apparently called a group of people "DIKS" in public.

"A vivid memory I have is when you were moderating focus groups and I was observing from behind the one-way mirror with others on our team. You introduced the session and said you were talking to two sets of people that night; the first group that you had already completed was with DINKS (those belonging to the dual-income no kids group) and now you were excited to be moderating the session with the DIKS (dual-income with kids group). The group stared at you and I was both laughing and crying when you said DIKS because as a newbie to this country, you really were completely unaware of what the term meant."

How and where did you grow up?

While we have been friends for a few decades now, and have had many conversations, I was still surprised at what a dialogue focused on her growing up years revealed.

Sue was born in Port Jervis, New York, a beautiful, small, lower-middle-class community outside New York City. Her dad was a kind man who came from a poor Jewish family and could not afford college. But he was a lifelong learner who went into the air force, became a butcher, and built the house Sue was born in. He managed the meat department in a small chain of grocery stores, and when the owner of the chain closed the stores with little notice, he went into business for himself. According to Sue, "*I did not meet anyone who did not like my father.*"

Sue's stay at home mom was the opposite of her dad and quite rigid. She was a very loving mom but had a very regimented schedule to be followed. She would do a designated task each day, finish her housework, serve lunch, and go out for a few hours. If anyone called when she was doing her housework, she would ask them to call back. While Sue's parents were not wealthy, her dad managed their money quite well, enabling them to take a two-week vacation each year.

What was your personality like as a child?

When I asked Sue to talk about her personality as a kid, she got a little sad and reminded me of how little insecurities can last a lifetime.

> "*My personality was formed as a result of being overweight as a child. My parents did not realize how damaging my brother saying "you are fat, you are stupid, you are ugly" was. It was not teasing, just a simple statement. The insecurity around my weight in my childhood is the biggest contributor to my lack of confidence as an adult. Since I dressed well, was fun to hang around, and smart, I was popular in school among both the academically successful group and the cool kids. In fact, to this day I remember one of my classmates from the cool side coming up to me and asking me if I was the Sue Morgenstern who was President of the Honors Society. The transition from childhood to adulthood scared me and I knew that I was going to be tested when I went away to college*".

What did you want to be when you grew up?

Sue's mom and aunt were into fashion. Her aunt owned a high-end clothing store, and that's how she became fascinated with dressing up. So, it is not surprising to hear that she wanted to be in the fashion business when she grew up.

"I wanted to be a fashion designer even though I did not think I had the creativity to do it. I was very good at taking ideas from many different places and putting things together, but not really great at generating ideas from scratch. I also had this idea that smart people study the sciences and the not so smart people studied the arts."

I was shocked to hear Sue say this, especially since I did not think that such sentiments about the arts and sciences existed outside of India. While Sue did become quite the fashionista, she ended up studying to be a mathematician and found her career in market research.

What did mealtimes look like when you were growing up? Any favorite food memories?

Sue is such a foodie like me, and despite not being a meat-eater, I enjoyed hearing about her early food forays. To Sue, food is associated with the words love, hate, pizza, ice cream, omnipresent, emotional crutch, cross-cultural, and hospitality.

"My mom cooked a hot dinner every night. The meal usually had meat (not a surprise since my father was a butcher), starch, and a vegetable. My dad and I, both had a sweet tooth. In our house, dessert was not served at dinner, but a little later in the evening. Food was a source of comfort for me. Whenever my brother's message played in my head and I needed consoling, food would serve as a crutch. To this day, I am a very emotional eater. Food is my companion when I am really happy or when I am really sad."

Besides the everyday dinners, Sue also dished out on her favorite meals during her growing up years.

> "I had a few absolute favorites. Mom used to make veal chops that were breaded and fried, and they were just delicious. Even though I make mine broiled, every time I eat veal chops, it brings back a flood of memories. I also loved salmon and called it an orange fish. I begged my dad to bring home orange fish and prime rib (a standing rib roast). Since Mom was a big fan of Italian food, I also loved all the dishes with sauces."

Can you share a favorite recipe of yours with me?

Sue and I share a sweet tooth and I was delighted to have her share a recipe for 'eat with less guilt' banana bread as her gift. Sue almost always has this banana bread in the house because it is made with whole wheat flour, no oil, apple sauce – good for you ingredients that make the bread super delicious as well. Needless to say, each time I make this banana bread, I will think of Sue.

What advice would you give to your younger self?

Reflecting back on her younger years, Sue said the one piece of advice she would give to her younger self is to *"Just go for it"*.

> "As a kid, I put too many limitations on myself; denied myself too much. I told myself that if I did not do something well, to just forget about it. And that led to a lot of missed opportunities."

What do you want your legacy in the world to be?

Sue expressed her legacy in five words.

"As a kind caring person."

SECTION 3
DIANE

State of mind: Excited about getting married and scared about the arrival of a competitor

It couldn't have been a happier period in my life. I was going back to India to get married to the guy I was paired up with in the Chemistry lab at 17. Given that it was a milestone period in my life, I requested and got a two-month leave of absence. And just as I was ready to pack up and leave, a bombshell announcement arrived. My boss had hired a new addition to the team who she termed as really sharp.

The insecurity wheels started churning in full motion. While my boss had said that I had the makings of an excellent researcher, would the new hire be better than me? Would I no longer be needed when I came back after getting married? Could I lose my job?

THE HIGH-FLYING DC GIRL

Have you ever met someone who you felt immediately was smarter than you, more talented than you, looked sharper than you, was more polished than you...the list could go on and on! Well, Diane fit that bill to a T. And **INSECURITY** was the screaming emotion I felt when I first heard about her.

She was joining the market research team at Verizon; a young, smart, savvy, business graduate who had some consulting experience under her belt. I'd been in my role as a market researcher for a couple of years and Diane sounded so much more qualified and capable than me, all of which rang true when I finally had the pleasure of meeting her.

While my recollection of our first meeting is hazy, one of our earliest interactions was at my wedding reception for friends and colleagues in the DC area. She was the consummate professional, neither bratty nor arrogant, and yet I felt antsy around her; a lingering nervousness would take hold that she would do a much better job than me and I could end up not being needed anymore, leaving me bereft of a job and that much-coveted American dream – a green card.

We were both part of a larger group of newbie professionals, all learning and trying to prove our mettle in the rapidly evolving telecommunications space while trying to get decent lunches within our limited means at places that were not named Taco Bell and Wendy's. So, when Delhi Dhaba opened up a stone's throw from our office, serving up delicious, hot Indian lunches with naan, vegetables, rice, and raita for under six bucks, the Flintstones phrase, "Yabba Dabba Do" became our lunchtime cry to indulge in an inexpensive yet filling meal. These lunches were filled with animated conversations around office gossip, food, renting vs. buying, the dating scene, things to do on weekends, and more, and these fun outings gradually turned Diane and me from acquaintances to good friends.

We bonded over tears and laughter, food and travel, cooking classes and shopping, and the joy and sadness of relationships. I learned that Diane's brother Tom had been killed by a drunk driver when she had just started college. Her sister was suffering from a mental illness. She herself had been diagnosed with a pretty serious health condition. The super polished, incredibly articulate, smart, and savvy Diane around whom I felt intimidated, was slowly evolving in my mind into a person I both admired and respected. Not only was she really good at her job, but she was one of the most positive, high energy people to be around, no matter the circumstances. From taking me to a diner for a celebratory birthday lunch when I was pregnant with my first child (the waiters sang while I attained bliss over a much-craved peanut butter sandwich) to making me take a stealth peek at the man she had a crush on (he is now her husband), from showing up to be with me within hours of my graduating to motherhood to joining me in learning to make lasagna roll ups professionally, our journey is peppered with an abundance of stories.

She may not know this, but my buddy Diane put me through finishing school and served as my in-house expert on truly transitioning to successful adulthood. You see, I was a country bumpkin when it came to understanding the nuances of working with the plethora of place settings routinely encountered at restaurants. Diane's table manners were impeccable – she mastered these skills at an early age and taught me how to navigate with sophistication. She also taught me a few other invaluable life skills - how you buy a house when you are far from rich, how you stay fit, how you take trips (beyond Disney) and, most of all, how you keep resilient. Oh, and can I add that she played a key role in me landing my dream job at Marriott!

It has been years since we first met. Two young women who went after life, work, and love with stars in their eyes, now beautifully settled on all three fronts; we took a common road and then diverged; the daily exchanges of life's highs and lows are history, but the friendship is anything but that.

A Q&A with Diane

What was your reaction to the tribute?

Diane, who works as a Senior Brand Executive at one of the top hospitality firms in the world, and lives in the Washington DC area with her husband, Peter, told me how she started crying when she read the tribute to her.

> *"I was overwhelmed and crying in a cab - but in a GOOD way. So many wonderful memories flooded over me. I was so grateful for this beautiful gift."*

When I heard Diane say this, it triggered so many of my own memories of our precious times together. However, Diane immediately disputed one aspect of my tribute.

> *"I was surprised that we all seem to assume we are the ONLY ones who are insecure. When I joined Verizon, I felt every bit as insecure about myself in your presence as you did with me. I had zero experience or expertise in Market Research, and you had tons. I asked a gazillion questions, you always had answers..."*

What was your favorite memory of our time together?

As I walked down my memory lane with Diane, I was curious to hear if our favorite recollections overlapped. She started with our meals at Delhi Dhaba and reminded me of ones that I had long forgotten.

> *"It has to start with the countless meals we shared at Delhi Dhaba! The location was an extremely unlikely setting for the foundation of our friendship. This is where I really fell in love with your laugh; my intellectual interest in history and geography turned into a deeper sensitivity to and appreciation for culture, and how it is expressed via food, family life, religion, customs, etc.; my interest in travel was transformed from a competitive sport of checking boxes, to wanting to really experience the places I visited so that I could understand them.*

Also, high up on the memory list was your shock when I explained that bathing suit sizes run one size small (a great conspiracy — how could you have known?), *hearing about your first experience at a gynecologist's office* (you never went to one till you were about to be married), *and your reaction to my first brow wax* (you only knew of threading)."

How and where did you grow up?

I wanted to learn more about how this native Washingtonian grew up to be so special and how being in the nation's capital might have woven its way into her life.

Diane was born and raised in the close-in suburbs of Washington DC, to two native Washingtonians. She was part of a normal, middle-class family; her mom stayed home to raise the three kids; her grandparents lived closed by, and Diane saw them often. In her words, *"It was a very suburban 70's upbringing where kids played in packs after school, roamed freely wherever they wanted as long as they were home on time for dinner; we did not have a fancy life, just a week in Ocean City each year for vacation."*

Growing up in the nation's capital infused another set of childhood memories - *"I remember the end of the Vietnam wars, gas lines, and Nixon resigning, but I didn't understand how much social change was happening around me."*

What was your personality like as a child?

When I asked Diane about her personality as a kid, I wasn't surprised by her response.

"I was highly self-motivated, a bit shy, sensitive, playful, upbeat, adaptable with a diverse group of friends. I defined myself by my smarts

and academic achievements and my parents never had to nag me to do my homework. I was lucky that both my parents made me really believe that I could do anything I put my mind to and worked hard for."

What did you want to be when you grew up?

In terms of thinking about a career, Diane had been in love with teaching from an early age, something that she has not shed to this day.

> *"I wanted to be a teacher when I grew up. Today, I think the reason I love doing presentations and speeches so much is that it brings out the teacher in me."*

Diane went on to study business in school, started her career in consulting, became a market researcher, and ended up as a Brand Executive for a global hospitality conglomerate.

What did mealtimes look like when you were growing up? Any favorite food memories?

Growing up in India, cooking was considered an integral part of motherhood and convenience foods were non-existent, especially for the middle class. My background made Diane's dinner time rituals truly sound from another world.

> *"My father came home from work, checked in with each kid, took a short nap and we ate at exactly 6:00 PM. You might have guessed, dinner was regimented. Tuesdays it was spaghetti, Thursdays we had hamburgers also known as "DooDoo Balls", and Saturdays we had special Salisbury steak that we referred to as leather patties.*
>
> *Dinner was really like a factory production line helmed by my mom who was an awful, passionless cook. Growing up with her parents and*

grandparents, she only learned to make brownies by the time she got married. Since it was the era of packaged, processed food, we got our vegetables as well as our favorite indulgences (TV Dinners or Chef Boyardee) from a frozen bag or can.

Before you roll your eyeballs, remember this all seemed normal at the time. And even with our regimented dinners and canned foods, there is something to be said about gathering together as a family EVERY night. We talked, we shared, we laughed."

By the time I met Diane, she was totally into her food. So, I was curious to hear about her favorite food experiences that might have influenced her later years.

"I can share a few. Both my grandmothers were great in the kitchen. My paternal grandmother was an outstanding baker; I can still smell, feel, and taste her pie crust and dinner rolls. My maternal grandmother would set dinner for 10 like it was nothing and make 15 different kinds of Xmas cookies each year. I learned the basics of how to cook from them.

Holiday dinners were always memorable because they not only brought joy from cooking and eating but also showed the positive social impact gathering around a meal can have. A really good family dinner was when the discussion got so lively and loud that my grandfather would sit back in his chair at the head of the table, turn down his hearing aid, and just smile and watch."

It comes as no surprise that today, Diane associates food with laughter, fun, intimacy, her dining room, and love.

Can you share a favorite recipe of yours with me?

Diane's gift to me was a recipe for her Rice Casserole, something she serves often to delighted friends and family. According to

Diane, "This is insanely easy and EVERYONE loves it. It also feeds a crowd and is fantastic for leftovers". I loved it when I tried it and making it will bring Diane virtually into my home every time.

What advice would you give to your younger self?

Like Marcia and Sue, Diane did not become what she thought she would. But given that she grew up as such a confident, self-assured young woman, did she have any advice for her younger self?

"Take more risks. I was pretty cautious and followed a lot of norms and prescribed notions. Some of that served me well, but I think I missed some fun and perhaps some opportunities. I'm not sure what I was afraid of, but I am a lot more fearless now. A good friend gave me a button which says - why ask 'why', when you can ask 'why not'? I wish I had embraced that sooner."

What do you want your legacy in the world to be?

Not having children, Diane struggles with the concept of legacy and how she wants to be remembered. It did not surprise me to hear that she wants to be remembered for who she was as a person and the impact she had on people, not by her career accomplishments.

"I hope my friends remember me as loyal, honest, positive, open-minded, energetic, and funny.

I hope my colleagues remember me as smart, strategic, supportive, direct, honest, and fair.

I hope my family remembers me as optimistic, adventuresome, loyal, practical, generous, and playful."

SECTION 4

MONA

S tate of mind: **Angry about moving, giving up my dream job, and being far away from family**

I absolutely loved and cherished living in the DC area. My parents and my grandmother lived down the street from me; they helped take care of my young baby whenever I had to work; I had good friends; I loved my favorite places to eat and chill; most of all, I had found my dream job at Marriott's headquarters and was traveling the world because of it.

But alas, things were not meant to last. My husband, upon completing his Ph.D., found a job a few states away, and after fretting, fuming, and commuting for a year, I decided to make the move permanent. I went from the hustle, bustle, and liveliness of city living to a home in the midst of farmlands, where I had to drive just to buy milk. I fought every aspect of the move and nothing felt right or good enough. While I landed a good job, I was back to being an outsider with no friends or family close by and facing the arduous task of forming new relationships from scratch.

THE WISDOM AND JOY INFUSER
FROM BOOKS AND BEYOND

For the 20 plus years I have known Mona, any challenge that we have discussed has usually led to this comment, *"You know Lakshmi, based on what I have read, the books say...".* This **WISDOM WHISPERER** has done this with such regularity that it has become a running joke between us, with me always asking, *"Mona, what do the books say about XYZ"?*

Advice from books is just a teeny-weeny part of the wisdom and joy that Mona has seeped into my life. I met her when I started my first job in health care at a company that had just been spun off into a new public entity. I had relocated from the DC area to New Jersey and immediately gravitated towards Mona, who lived in my former hometown and also commuted to New Jersey. We became quick friends and just a few months later, Mona joined me on the first of many milestone moments we would end up sharing; she turned "official photographer" for my four-year old's birthday celebration at pre-school.

. . .

Each time Mona came up north or I went down south, we would meet up and share little nuggets from our lives. Her conservative Palestinian upbringing in some ways paralleled my formative years in a traditional Indian family. There were important pre-defined roles/rules for women and getting married within the community was one of them. In a windowless conference room over laughter and tears, Mona shared the story of how she had met a young lawyer who absolutely cherished her, who was not Palestinian, was biracial, and how she felt ripped apart about having to make a choice between her parents, her community, and the man she had grown to love. I was blown away by her implicit trust, openness, vulnerability, and complete lack of hang-ups. We lived through the journey of her doubts, her ulti-mate decision to be with the man she loved, her parental disap-proval, their disappearance till the birth of her first child, and the anxiety, nervousness, and sadness that at times tinged some of her life's happiest milestone moments.

While Mona was going through these challenges, I was going through my own set of life changes - the death of my father-in-law, the permanent move of my mother-in-law to live with us, a situation that led to our extended family moving in with us for eight months, an increasingly hectic work travel schedule for my husband and, of course, me trying to balance an intense work life with the demands of raising our children. She may not realize this, but my phone calls with Mona during this time were the perfect balm for my weary soul.

If it sounds like our friendship was all seriousness and no fun, nothing could be further from the truth. As a new homeowner, I remember inviting Mona to dinner, getting gutsy, and deciding to make falafels instead of my well-tried Indian meals. As Mona watched, each falafel I dropped into the oil disintegrated into pieces, leading to an SOS call to her mom, who guided us on resurrecting our meal. Mona was also one of the first members of our team to get into the internet start-up space and enthusiastically asked us to check out her new employer's website. In our excitement, we ended up one alphabet off, getting on to an adult website instead and spending days fearing that we would be fired upon being discovered. More recently, we bonded over our mutual love for Trevor Noah, joining other friends to watch live tapings of his show, heartily laughing our way through these experiences.

Mona and I started our life journeys on different continents and grew up pushing through some of the societal/cultural boundaries set for us – we both worked in professional jobs outside the home, got married to guys who were not picked by our parents, traveled the world by ourselves, and grew our families through the less culturally common practice of adoption. The last act was one which brought us even closer.

I could not be more grateful for how our friendship has evolved over time. For years, Mona and I have not lived in close proximity to one another. We have caught up in sporadic conversations, every impromptu phone call or planned meet up taking off into the serious and lighthearted happenings in our lives without a moment of awkwardness or pause. But lately, with each of us dealing with a parent battling dementia, our conversations have become more frequent, emotional, and intense. And I know this for sure – no matter where in the world Mona might live, she has turned into a "friend sister" who will always be just a phone call away.

. . .

A Q&A with Mona

What was your reaction to the tribute?

Mona, the "energizer bunny" mom who lives in Connecticut with her husband and three kids had this reaction to her tribute.

> *"I read this when you first sent it to me and reread it before our call for the interview. I am absolutely in awe of how accurately you captured our friendship. You have so eloquently touched on the various aspects of our friendship and what makes it so special. Thank you for your insights and memories. As I read through this, it made me recall our journey together and brought back many fond memories."*

I laughed fondly with Mona as we recalled our precious times together.

What was your favorite memory of our time together?

Mona and I have shared so many laughs and tears together, that I needed to hear her favorite recollection of them. It centered around a move in her life that did not happen.

> *"One of my favorites is when Jordan and I were contemplating a transition from the DC area to New Jersey. You had made a similar move and opened your home and heart to us as we explored our options in the area. Just being in your home, being able to voice my uncertainties, and hearing about your experiences made the situation so much better and helped me be so much calmer. Let me not forget to add that my kids loved being in your home and driving the kiddie scooter around. They felt like they were in Disneyland!"*

How and where did you grow up?

Over the years, we have spoken about our cultural similarities; yet I found a walk down her childhood memory lane both fascinating and revealing.

Mona grew up in a middle class, Palestinian family in Elyria, a small town near Cleveland, Ohio. Her father studied engineering at the University of Maryland and worked as an engineer for GM; her mom was a teacher in Bethlehem and Kuwait and moved to the United States after marrying her dad. Mona's mom stayed home to raise her and her three brothers and handled all the cooking, cleaning, and other housework. Her childhood memories had some indelible moments.

"Even though my parents were welcomed with open arms by all of our neighbors and the town, I was very aware that we were the only Arabs in town. I was so embarrassed that my mom would speak Arabic 24x7 which made it very obvious that we were not locals. Another thing that made us different was our food. My mom cooked a lot of middle eastern food and back then no one was familiar with middle eastern food like they are now. My mom made the best, stuffed grape leaves. I remember going to pick grape leaves with my mom at the edge of a freeway every year. As we tucked the grape leaves into our plastic bags, my eyes would scan the area, fearful that one of my friends would catch me indulging in this strange act. I used to pick them as fast as I could so that we could hurry up and leave."

What was your personality like as a child?

Mona talked about how the freedom and restrictions of growing up in a conservative family shaped her personality.

"I was a happy go lucky kid who had friends. I was both bossy and a rule follower. But there was one thing that made me feel very self-

conscious and that was my skin color. I was darker than all the kids around me and even though my friends completely accepted me, I felt uncomfortable with how I looked.

"I honestly don't remember a lot of girl drama when I was growing up. I loved dancing and the release of Saturday Night Fever only pushed me to want to dance even more. I would tell my parents that I was going to the movies with my friends and instead of heading to the cinema we would go dancing at the local night club. While that might make me appear to be a rule-breaker, I was actually very appreciative and respectful of the freedom my parents gave me. Being educated, my parents supported me and gave me more freedom than the other Arab families that we knew in Cleveland. Even though they were strict with me and did not give me nearly the freedom that my American friends had, I knew that it could be much worse if I was in another Arab family. Since I valued this freedom so much, I was careful to not do anything that they would disapprove of, such as having a boyfriend, drinking, or smoking. I knew that if I did those things and got caught, I would lose the privileges I had."

What did you want to be when you grew up?

As a kid, every time I was asked the question, "What do you want to be when you grow up?", I was embarrassed to admit that I had no clue. When the same question was posed to my kids, I was annoyed that the world expected answers from them so early on. Mona's thoughts on what she wanted to be kept shifting over time.

"My earliest memories of what I wanted to be when I grew up was a teacher. In college, I took a semester of education classes, and as a student taught second graders. It was then that I knew that I was not cut out to be a teacher; I did not have the necessary patience. Next, I took some

nursing pre-requisites but quickly realized that I was not a fan of blood and gore. I kept waiting for the 'magic major' to hit me the way it did for so many of my peers, but it never did. Ultimately, it was my father who urged me to study a discipline that required a license such as medicine, law, engineering, architecture or accounting where my job could not be outsourced easily to anyone. So, I majored in accounting and became a CPA."

Mona started her career working for Arthur Anderson, a big eight accounting firm, and went on to work in senior roles in health care and financial services before becoming a super-duper full-time mom.

What did mealtimes look like when you were growing up? Any favorite food memories?

Mealtimes in Mona's childhood reminded me a lot of mine. My mom did all the work, we ate food from a few parts of India, and we did not have many conversations while doing so. As Mona replayed her childhood dinners, she also reflected on certain oddities she discovered later in life when she had her own family.

"We always had dinner together as a family. Mom cooked mostly middle eastern food, set the table, and did all of the clean-up after dinner. We did not have assigned chores and my mom never really expected us to help out around the house unless we were having guests. As a wife and mother now, I feel bad that my mom shouldered all the burden and yet never complained.

At mealtimes, there wasn't a lot of discussion around the table. My siblings and I fought a bit, complained about who was kicking whom under the table, but never really about our day or what was going on at school. Often, when we would start to have a conversation, my dad would say that it was time to eat and not talk. I guess he did not understand the importance of connecting with one another at mealtimes, probably because that was how he was raised.

I never shared anything with my brothers, we did not talk much, we were friendly but not friends and honestly, I did not think any of this was abnormal till I had my own kids. For the first several years, I marveled at how well my kids played together and how much fun they always had."

I asked Mona if she had any special food memories outside of the everyday meals. Her family really lived the spirit of Thanksgiving.

"I'll share a few. Thanksgiving was always the most special meal, both for the food and the meaning my mom infused into the celebration. My mom is a very likable woman who had many friends across different age groups. She always invited people who could not be home with their own families to partake in our Thanksgiving meal. There was an older couple (a Turkish man and his American wife) who my parents met at the mosque, and they would join us as would another American couple who were college professors actively involved in advocating for issues in Palestine. When my brothers went away to college, they would often bring home their Palestinian friends who did not have family close by.

For our Thanksgiving meal, we would have a traditional home-cooked American spread with the largest turkey my mom could find, green bean casserole, sweet potatoes, mashed potatoes, corn, cranberry sauce, and pumpkin pie alongside traditional Arab dishes like Hashweh (rice and meat stuffing). Mom would also bake a lot of bread and deliver it to friends and neighbors.

Another special memory is the six times a year we went out to eat to celebrate each of our birthdays. Those trips were usually to Sweden House for their all you can eat buffet or to Ponderosa for their steak. Occasionally, there would be a McDonald's treat thrown in. Other than that, we rarely ate out."

Can you share a favorite recipe of yours with me?

Since hummus is an all-time favorite dish of mine, I was super excited to hear that it was one of Mona's specialties. She gets rave reviews from whoever she makes it for. Her secret ingredient, whole milk plain yogurt, adds tanginess, smoothness, and richness. This will be on repeat in my kitchen to keep Mona vibes flowing.

What advice would you give to your younger self?

As I asked each friend what advice she would give to her younger self, I was surprised by the similarity in the themes that emerged. This is what Mona had to say.

> *"I would tell myself to worry less about what people think and focus on being true to myself and doing what feels right to me. I would give myself the freedom to 'just be' and tell myself that you cannot make everyone happy all the time. At the end of the day, you have to look at yourself in the mirror and be comfortable with who you are and the choices you make.*
>
> *I have a little story to share here. My college roommate, who died of cancer would ask me, "why does everything about you involve aibe (shame/culturally inappropriate) or haram (God would be displeased if he saw you doing something bad)"? She was right; for so much of my life, aibe and haram were guideposts to how I lived."*

What do you want your legacy in the world to be?

So many of us spend our lives seeking and building professional success. Yet, once again, I heard a request for a legacy defined by human values.

"I want people to remember me as a kind, honest, loyal, loving, friend, mother, and wife. As someone who helped others and brought light and joy to the people she was around."

State of mind: Hoping to connect with other moms and find a mom-friend

Slowly but surely, I had reluctantly come to accept that we were not returning back to the DC area. As a mom with a career, life was pretty crazy. Still, I wanted to connect with other working moms to share perspectives and hopefully gain some new friends along the way. While having a kid made connecting with other moms easy, especially since we crossed paths at daycare, school, and more, finding a mom who could be a close friend was a tougher challenge to conquer. There were lots of little chats I had with other moms around kids, schools, birthdays, babysitters, and more, but only a handful of conversations that veered towards who we were as working women and the challenges we faced on a daily basis. Aah! I had been here so many times in my life before...trying to find a friend in a world where everyone appeared to have long-lasting friendships since grade school.

A SOUL SISTER FROM ANOTHER
MOTHER

BRILLIANCE – It was the brilliance of her smile that stayed with me long after I first bumped into her, rushing in, dressed in a navy blue maternity dress to pick up her four-year-old at the daycare center our kids attended.

We kept crossing paths over the years as we attended school events and shopped for groceries. Slowly, the casual hellos grew into conversations about kids, parents, spouses, careers, the struggle to manage it all, and more. Over time, I slowly discovered the depth of brilliance of this super talented woman whose middle name could aptly be humility. She studied at Princeton, traveled around the globe, fell in love in China with a guy who did not even share a common language, wrote a book about their romance, reinvented herself professionally from an investor to an executive recruiter to a middle school history teacher. All in one incredibly rich life, and I think she is a long way from being done.

Our life journeys started differently. She was raised in a middle-class, Jewish home in Chicago, grew up in one place as a kid, and went to school to pursue a degree in International Relations. I was raised in a middle class, Hindu home in India, moving to a new city every few years, and eventually chose to pursue a degree in Chemistry. She chose a path of adventure in her youth; I took the more conservative route... And yet when we reflect on our shared similarities, big and small, we think providence had a role in bringing together two sisters from different mothers.

Our kids shared the same schools, classes, and activities. Our curious mothers saved newspaper clippings of thought-provoking stories to share with us. Our spouses hold PhDs in similar fields of Chemistry and embarked on non-traditional work adventures around the same time, shuttling between the US and China for many, many years. Each of us single-handedly managed a lot of the day to day trials and tribulations of raising young, opinionated girls as our daughters. This list could go on and on.

In the last two decades, Bess has evolved from being the mother of my kids' friends to someone who just gets me at every level. We have celebrated surviving our kids' teenage angsts, cried over the loss of her mom, screamed with joy over our kids getting into their dream schools, rolled our eyeballs about our spouses refusing to see doctors, lamented the loss of a daily partner when our spouses were absent, and laughed over how we continue to somehow appear so pulled together when the world around us is falling apart.

. . .

Among laughter and tears, bagels and Indian food, Bess has provided me with some invaluable wisdom. Here are a few snippets...

When I nagged my playful younger daughter to take school more seriously, Bess reminded me: *"Lakshmi, no matter what, you have to preserve the relationship you have with your child. At no stage can the stress of school or performance ever come in the way of that."*

As I shared my experiences living with my mother-in-law over the last twenty years, Bess would remind me to focus on myself a tad bit more: *"You have to nourish your soul and keep yourself sane. You need to make you a priority."*

When I struggled to sometimes give the right guidance to my kids, Bess would say: *"It's good to get a therapist. The right one can make a world of difference in providing an objective perspective."*

Many of our meetings end with Bess and me talking with much optimism and fondness about our future - growing old together, saving enough money, learning, taking trips, spending more time with our spouses, and of course never letting go of our soulful, enriching exchanges over bagels and Indian food.

A Q&A with Bess

What was your reaction to the tribute?

Bess is a passionate middle school history teacher who lives in suburban New Jersey with her spouse, who still commutes between New Jersey and China. Bess, a proud mother of two accomplished daughters, had this to say about my tribute.

> *"Oh my gosh Lakshmi, I was absolutely blown away! I also thought this is just so beautiful and honestly such a worthwhile project. I am not really surprised by anything. And that is because we have connected at such a deep level. It also reminded me of a regret I had – not really knowing my friends and where they came from. So much of my life, I was so centered on myself; I forgot to ask people who they were. Since then, I have gone back and tried to fix that."*

I turned a bit teary hearing that my words had touched her heart in this special way.

What was your favorite memory of our time together?

Bess did not have one memorable recollection to share. She shared how every memory blended with another to show the growth of our friendship.

> *"I can't say it is one memory. It feels like it is a series of memories that have always been about us being together and sharing our lives. We are all messy people who live in a world where people see and share their well-curated sides. I have always felt safe sharing that messy self with you; I have always felt that you treasure who I genuinely am."*

How and where did you grow up?

Bess was born in an upper-middle-class suburb north of Chicago that was known for its beautiful lawns, homes, and excellent schools. It was a stretch for her middle class, Jewish parents to afford to live there, but they wanted their kids to have access to the best education.

"My father started his career working in the family optical business but chose to become a stockbroker to have more time with his young family. My mom was a teacher turned homemaker. I arrived as the much-heralded treasure to complete our family, joining my older brothers Joey, six, and Peter, five. True to the meaning of the word treasure, I was spoiled!

I have so many lovely memories of growing up. It was such a safe and happy existence. I would walk home from school, run barefoot across the family lawn and Charlie who helped my mom with the kids was there to greet me. I always remember the fun we had outdoors. On hot, Independence Day celebrations, the sprinklers would be going, dad would raise the flag and we would say our pledge of allegiance; in the winters, dad would build a fire and we would all sit outside like we were camping. And then there was the spying! My girlfriend Suzie Stone and I loved reading Harriet the Spy and we were so inspired that we would carry notebooks and magnifying glasses and peer into people's homes.

Most of all, I remember our family being happy together and that had a huge impact on me when I grew up."

What was your personality like as a child?

Over the years, everything I heard from Bess about her childhood had a blissful ring to it. Yet, when we sat down to take a walk down memory lane, I was surprised to get a peek into her insecurities and taken aback to see the similarities they shared with mine.

"When I was little, all I wanted was to be with my mom. In fact, my mom and I were inseparable. We did everything together – we read, we sang, and I sat glued to her lap during my frequent ear infections as she clipped away newspaper articles. When I started nursery school, I

sobbed every day because I did not want to be separated from my mom. When I got a bit older, I would go with my mom to see rehearsals of famous bands like Peter, Paul, and Mary; we could never afford the concerts, but the rehearsals were always free. Music was an important part of my life. On summer camping vacations, I sat in the back of our car with mom, singing songs from our songbooks; and because I loved to sing, Peter would make up songs as we walked to school so we could sing together.

I was largely an extrovert and always wanted to chat with people. While I made close friends, I struggled to relate to them because they were so wealthy. They had extravagant vacations to far-flung places and their moms had beautiful hair and perfectly done nails. To keep up, I kept altering my five tops so that it did not appear that I only had a few pieces of clothing. I felt like an outsider and to this day some of that sentiment has stayed with me."

What did you want to be when you grew up?

Bess wanted to be many things when she grew up. And while she may not have become every one, she is one woman who has reinvented herself many times over her life.

"I wanted to be so many things. When I was 12, I stood on our green carpet and drew out a plan; I was going to go to Scripps college to study oceanography, I was going to travel to all the different countries in the world, buy clothes, and then I was going to be Secretary of State.

My fascination with nature continued over the years as did my interest in foreign policy which led me to the Woodrow Wilson School and on to an internship at the State Department. Oh, and when I went away to college, I thought I wanted to go into theatre, but by the time I got to my sophomore year, I realized that only the upper crust of society went to theaters and I lost interest."

Bess studied a few different disciplines, worked in a few different careers, and today derives her joy from getting her middle schoolers to debate and think through the happenings of American history beneath a beautiful poster of Frederick Douglass.

What did mealtimes look like when you were growing up? Any favorite food memories?

To Bess, food is synonymous with her mom, matzo balls, and her grandma who was an amazing cook. Bess and I share a love for starch, but certainly not meat. I loved hearing about how dinner time took on a special routine for Sabbath and laughed when I heard about the accompanying conversations.

> *"We always had dinner together. Mom cooked unless it was summer when dad barbecued. We had a lot of meat. Apparently, when I was a kid, I would pound on the high chair...steak, steak! There was always starch. Mom would say, "Bessie is always starch on starch". On Friday nights for Sabbath, we would say our prayers over the challah; I felt so honored to sing the song for the family and it made me feel that I mattered.*
>
> *What I cherish the most about those dinners were the conversations we had around the table. We actually thought that we could rent out Carnegie Hall and people would pay to listen to our dinner time debates and arguments about a multitude of topics, especially around civil rights. These meals also made me feel that I always had a voice at the table."*

Bess also recalled several memorable food moments from family celebrations in her childhood.

> *"Capon and roast chicken for Sabbath, especially soaking up all the gravy with the challah was just very special. The other favorite meal was our celebration for New Years. We would pull up the dining room*

table to the fireplace, decorate the table, bring out our big "happy" handmade sign, and have lobsters and clam. I especially loved dipping lobster in the butter.

Fast forward many years, and we still bring out our "happy" sign, but our dipping sauce has taken on an East meets West flavor since the addition of Rouxin (Bess's husband). We now dip the lobster in a yummy concoction made with soy sauce, scallion, ginger, and Chinese vinegar."

Can you share a favorite recipe of yours with me?

Bess shared a recipe for her Cold Tofu with Scallions, a dish that will always bring a whiff of her and Rouxin's romance into my life. When she was a newlywed, she lived with Ruoxin in the Beijing hotel and both of them ordered this dish from the dining room almost every day.

What advice would you give to your younger self?

Bess paused to reflect on the advice she would give to her younger self.

"Don't feel bad about feeling like an outsider. It's okay to be who you are. The you that you are is enough.

As confident as I was, the piece of me that felt like an outsider always wondered what's wrong with me and why I could not fit in. Today, I would not want to be anyone else."

What do you want your legacy in the world to be?

Bess has no doubt about what she wants her legacy to be.

"*I want to be remembered as someone who was kind and who cared about other people. I see so much horror in the world. As a teacher, I see my kids impacted by selfishness and manipulation. Some of them come back and tell me that they are so grateful that I cared. And that's all I want.*"

SECTION 6
ANITA

State of mind: At my wits end due to repeat visits to the principal's office

It started right when my youngest daughter entered kindergarten and met Nic – they became the best of friends and a formidable trouble making duo. I could not believe that two kids could be so similar. And each time I was summoned to the principal's office, Nic was there with his mom.

My older kid was a rule follower in her early years and going to the principal's office on a regular basis was not only a new experience for me, but it was also annoying and embarrassing. I was at my wit's end, trying a variety of approaches to change the situation, meeting with little success. I thought Nic's mom could help me navigate this unfamiliar terrain.

A PRECIOUS GIFT FROM
TWINNING TROUBLE MAKERS

I can't think of Anita without thinking about the **twinning troublemakers** that got us together in the first place. Anita's son and my younger daughter added new meaning to the words, "gifts that keep on giving". Over the years, Anita and I were awarded with repeat visits to teachers' and principals' offices to do what Ricky Ricardo called some "splainin to do". There wasn't a year through these kids' elementary and middle school years where we were not summoned multiple times. As we became acquainted with each other, our kids became the best of friends, turning into constant fixtures in each other's homes and lives.

It is hard to pinpoint when our regular bump-ins and exchanges transcended into a deeper friendship; when our eyeball rolling conversations about our kids' never-ending antics, transformed into growing open, honest, judgment-free discussions on many things.

I think three annual traditions and one reliable espresso machine certainly played their part in bringing us closer - Anita and her husband Bob's annual summer barbecue, their post-Thanksgiving dessert routine, and my daughter Sathya's joint birthday celebrations with her sister, Siddhi, which attracted dozens of kids. At these celebrations, Anita and I spoke about our shared challenges as working parents, our dream of "normalcy" for our kids (which to us meant not being summoned to school every other day), little stories on our respective careers, and the beginning of a long journey talking about food. But it was when Anita lost her job and I lost mine a few years later that my trusted Delonghi machine poured forth the cappuccinos that fueled our lengthy, candid exchanges on a variety of topics ranging from the serious to the light-hearted.

We shared notes on our youth; she in a tiny apartment in New York City, the only child of frugal, disciplined, immigrant, Italian parents, and me in a middle-class home in Mumbai. We talked about our experiences commuting to college for our undergraduate degrees. We laughed about our shared insecurity around money with an ongoing paranoia of ending up back where we started. We traded stories of how we met our spouses – she met hers through a mutual friend, the sparks flying over their smarts, love for dancing, food, and of course a desire to make a difference. We talked about in-laws – I shared bits and bytes of mother-in-law episodes and she reminisced about her in-laws with whom she was barely connected. We laughed with childlike enthusiasm when the conversation veered to food, coffee, recipes, new finds at Trader Joe's, and more. We animatedly debated the pressures on school kids, the dysfunctionalities in the health care system, and the blatant discrimination in work and life. We giggled about our mutual admiration for a local physician who not only checked the boxes on being an outstanding doctor with impeccable manners but also got better looking with every interaction. When we ended our meetups, there was always more to talk about.

More recently, Anita and I have gone off on day-long adventures, sampling chocolate, drinking unlimited cups of coffee at food festivals, and providing fuel for the brain by attending multiple TEDx sessions.

Sometimes, an inciting incident leads to the growth of a friendship. In our case, a seed planted by the antics of two mischievous friends grew into a beautiful tree, whose branches represent the many dimensions over which Anita and I have bonded over the last 16 years. The trunk of this tree is a perfect analogy for what Anita stands for – a solid, unwavering, watching my back presence in my life. A friend whose most powerful life lesson to me is to be myself unabashedly. Anita speaks her mind without political niceties and gives me her honest take on situations. She shares things that are happening in her life as they are, no sugar coating necessary. She takes her responsibility as a friend very seriously and is there for me through the small, big, and most important moments. She does not believe in soft-spoken expressions of love, joy, or anger - she shows her feelings. And she wears her grey with pride and dances with abandon when the music is turned on.

Over the years, Anita has texted me and sent me notes to tell me that it is a privilege to be called my friend. But the truth is, the privilege is all mine – to have this force of a friend called Anita be a constant in my life.

A Q&A with Anita

· · ·

What was your reaction to the tribute?

Anita, an Associate Teaching Professor at Rutgers University lives with her husband Bob in suburban New Jersey. She attributes her grays and her laugh lines to parenting Nic, (a young adult), and Jennie, (a teen trying to turn adult). This is how she reacted to my tribute.

> *"Okay, I cried the first time I read this. I had to go and make a cup of tea and sit and read and reread this. I don't make friends easily. I can be tough and unapproachable and I don't like to pretend so that often puts people off. So true friendship is a gift."*

And I cried, grateful that Anita felt the same way about our friendship.

What was your favorite memory of our time together?

Given our long journey together, I was very curious to know if Anita's favorite memories of us aligned with mine.

> *"I have to say it has to be on how on-point we were at the Coffee Festival. We were so in sync that it was almost like having a twinning experience!"*

How and where did you grow up?

While Anita and I have shared many stories about our lives, this journey gave me an opportunity to learn more about her.

· · ·

Anita grew up as an only child to Italian, immigrant parents in New York City. Her dad worked as a barber and her mom was a seamstress. Anita's mom had hearing challenges and after a surgery lost most of her hearing and could not work anymore. I've known Anita for many years, but this was the first time I heard her use the word "tough" to describe her youth.

"What I never realized was how tough it was growing up in New York City. Everyone was hard-working, and everyone watched everyone else. If you did something wrong, the whole neighborhood knew and that was why you got into twice as much trouble with your parents. We were poor and I really never knew how poor until much later. I do know that it was pushed very hard on me to get an education, to get into college and make something of myself. I spent a lot of time alone, so I read. The library was my favorite place in the world! "

What was your personality like as a child?

Anita is able to have conversations with people across all age groups and interests. She even has conversations with my husband, who does not like to socialize. So, I was surprised to hear that Anita did not have a lot of friends growing up.

"Even as a child, I was always talkative. Since my mother was partially deaf, I had to spend a lot of time explaining things to her. I was always outgoing, though I didn't have a lot of friends. I didn't make friends that easily. That was hard."

What did you want to be when you grew up?

Prior to working on this tribute, I had never asked Anita what she wanted to be when she grew up. So, it was fun for me to hear about her childhood dreams.

"For the longest time, I wanted to be an astronaut. However, you needed perfect vision to qualify. When I learned I would not make it in because I wore glasses, I started to think more about doing research in the sciences. I really wanted to search for new things and move new ideas forward."

True to her dream of moving new things/ideas forward, Anita went on to get her Ph.D. from Columbia University. She worked on many aspects of health care design and delivery and is now channeling her rich trove of experiences to train the next generation of thinkers/problem solvers.

What did mealtimes look like when you were growing up? Any favorite food memories?

Given that Anita mentioned growing up poor, it is not a surprise that meals in the Franzione household were simple.

"We had simple meals at home. My father worked late hours and my mom never ate until my dad got home from work. So, I ate my dinners alone before dad came home pretty much until high school. We ate together as a family on Sundays. Since we could not eat before church, we had breakfast around 11 am and our main meal was around 3 – 3:30 pm. We always had salads at every meal and fruit after dinner. Cakes and desserts never made an appearance after a meal."

While everyday meals might have been simple, Anita did experience her fair share of celebrations. In fact, food to her is all about fun, adventure, and sharing.

"Whenever we celebrated an event, from big ones like weddings and baptisms to smaller ones like holidays and birthdays, it was always lots of people and lots of food because (true to Italian sensibilities) heaven forbid, the food ran out. There was lots of noise, abundant talking, and

getting up and down from the table. Now that I look back at it, I can't imagine how it was done. But there is one big thing that I remember very clearly - if anyone showed up, there was always room at the table."

Even after a big celebration, there would always be someone asking whether you needed something else to eat.

"One of my aunts would always come out after cleaning up after an event saying "Anyone hungry? I can make you a sandwich!" Because the sandwiches were a snack, not a meal. It was something to hold you until the next meal or to get you to bed."

Can you share a favorite recipe of yours with me?

True to her Italian heritage, Anita shared a recipe for her favorite soup – Pasta e Fagioli. Since meat was not eaten on Fridays and other holy days, Anita ate a lot of vegetarian food and this recipe was a particular favorite made by pure memory and taste. The fact that you can create this soup with a bit of this and a bit of that means that it will be making an appearance in my kitchen quite often.

What advice would you give to your younger self?

Given her completely practical nature, Anita had some pragmatic advice for her younger self.

"Yes, it is going to be a hard and bumpy road ahead of you. But with each fall, each mistake, each suffering, you will come out stronger and be able to fulfill your dream – making a difference to others. And there will be people, good people, alongside you."

What do you want your legacy in the world to be?

In terms of her legacy, she wants to be remembered in a very simple way.

> *"I want to be remembered as someone who made a difference in this world."*

SECTION 7

IRIS

State of mind: **Super excited at the thought of joining a startup team**

I had been in my role in my company in New Jersey for a few years when the internet started exploding. Our firm spun off a division to focus on how the internet could revolutionize clinical trials and I wanted to be part of it. When I approached the head of this new division, he told me to reach out to a highly respected leader to see if there would be a possibility of me joining the team. Mona was already part of this exciting new venture and I was excited at the prospect of working with her and others who had stellar reputations within the company. Unlike them, my experience in the healthcare space was limited, and the chance of me landing a position on this amazingly competitive team was slim to none.

THE PERFECTIONIST, ROCKING CHEERLEADER

 **PERFECTIONIST** – That is the first word that comes to mind when I think of Iris. She was the perfect boss, made the perfect quilts, decorated the perfect home...and of course, she was one of the biggest cheerleaders to my non-perfectionist soul.

Iris and I met a few decades ago when she hired me into the new start-up arm of an established drug development organization. A few minutes after our informal interview, Iris quietly announced that she trusted me to add value to the team. Really? Have any of you heard the word trust used so soon after a first meeting? It made me want to do my best for a woman who had so much faith in me and my abilities. That theme continues to this day; whenever I go through a phase of self-doubt or insecurity, Iris will wave her confidence-boosting wand at me – I trust you; you are talented, you can do so many things if you just let yourself go.

. . .

While our relationship might have started in a boss-employee capacity, Iris soon became a friend, inspirer, and cheerleader. Like me, Iris grew up overseas (in Germany) and moved to the US as a young adult. She also married an introvert and we frequently joked about our weekends being centered around long conversations with our spouses. We had kids around the same age and shared stories about the craziness of parenting. Any talk of Kinder eggs (a European chocolate treat) brought smiles to our faces and while we both loved good food, Iris did not believe in slaving away for hours in the kitchen to have a meal disappear within minutes. Her joy came from creating her perfectly decorated home, designing flawless quilts, handling home redesign projects with aplomb, and generally speaking being meticulous with everything she took on.

And yet, Iris's life was far from perfect. An attic fire burned her beautifully designed home to the ground. At the same time, her middle child had mental health challenges which resulted in beyond scary moments as a parent. It was the way she recovered from these situations that led her to become my inspiration. Left facing the rubble of her beautiful home, Iris set about educating herself about all aspects of a rebuild. From the right tiles to the perfect toilet, from the best fixtures to paints that last, Iris learned every little nuance and detail. She became so well versed in building and decorating that she went back to school to transform herself into an interior designer. She started her own design firm that went from humble staging assignments to doing massive, interior re-dos of luxury homes. She learned to design websites and worked with branding consultants to further expand her business. Each of these a remarkable feat achieved by a woman who for years specialized in managing complex programs to bring new medicines to market. And as far as her kids go, she was an incredible mom to all three of them, fostering the adventure-seeking older son, handholding her middle one through his challenging years, and forming the much-awaited mother-daughter bond with her youngest. One of the most beautiful testaments to Iris as a mom came from her daughter, who said she wished she had been born much earlier so she would have that many more years with her amazing mother.

The part of Iris that has and will always be a constant in my life is her presence as a cheerleader. As a boss, she sought perfection from herself and others and got it by being an excellent coach, a creative problem solver, and an incredible listener. She asked for my input, went batting for me with unconventional approaches, and most of all kept pushing me to show off my talents with confidence rather than with an overdose of humility. She encouraged me to consult independently, gave wings to my fledgling writing talent, and lent support to my creative ideas. Every time I came close to making the decision to cut the umbilical cord of corporate life and chickened out, Iris would reinforce how I was not being true to my talents. Thanks to that support, I finally took the plunge to not only consult independently but also started writing more regularly.

Like other dear friends, Iris and I are now separated by thousands of miles. Yet, the connection remains, and I can't wait to visit her in her not so new home in Arizona and cook a meal in her perfectly designed kitchen!

A Q&A with Iris

What was your reaction to the tribute?

My dear friend Iris is a multitalented woman who lives in her somewhat new state of Arizona with her husband. True to her Germanic roots, Iris's feedback to every question I posed was very factual and brief. When I asked her about her reaction to the tribute, she had this to say.

> *"I was so honored and flattered. I had a big smile on my face because I can't believe some of the details you remembered, like the Kinder eggs; I remembered so many of our discussions after reading your comments."*

This compliment from Iris made me smile.

What was your favorite memory of our time together?

Iris is such an introvert, a thinker, and a woman of few words. So, when I asked about her cherished memory of our times together, it elicited a pretty deep response.

> *"It is actually a set of memories around being in the company of a circle of strong women (of which you were a part). We were part of a confident group that supported one another, taught each other, and were simply fun to be around.*
>
> *With each and every encounter we had, whether professional or personal, I always felt that I learned something, or my horizon was expanded. There was never even a tinge of jealousy or competition and we had nothing but full trust and respect for each other.*
>
> *I have to add here that as much as you were lacking confidence for yourself at times, you were always confident about us which was greatly appreciated."*

Like Diane, Iris also expressed surprise at my complexes.

> *"I was surprised and taken aback to read that you were intimidated by me. In fact, I always felt like an uneducated "fraud" in comparison to you! Isn't that something?"*

How and where did you grow up?

Iris was born and raised in Germany and grew up trying to stake her place in a home with three, boisterous younger brothers. And just like me, she moved around a lot.

> *"My parents were very strict, frugal, and moved every two years which was very tough for me because I was an extremely shy girl. Since I was in the minority as a girl, I mostly had boy toys growing up and remember playing a lot with Legos. Despite my shyness, I was 'tough' since I had to stand up to my brothers, babysitting them, etc."*

What was your personality like as a child?

When asked about her personality as a kid, Iris had just one statement to make – *"I was a very shy kid."* This shy theme has been a constant in her life and as an adult when Iris undertook personality tests, she was always classified as an introvert.

What did you want to be when you grew up?

Iris's introverted personality coupled with societal/parental expectations created an interesting dilemma for her with future aspirations.

> *"I always thought that it would be really interesting to become an architect. However, I never verbalized those ideas to my parents. Our parents kind of had the expectation that each of us would study engineering, science, etc. My stepfather, who I grew up with, was an engineer and all three of my brothers became engineers. I could not imagine pursuing something completely different.*

These beliefs were so deep-rooted, that even when I went back to school in my early 50s to study Interior Design, I was afraid at first to tell my mother!"

Iris went on to study the sciences, worked for years in the pharmaceutical industry, before returning to her passion for buildings and homes by becoming an interior designer.

What did mealtimes look like when you were growing up? Any favorite food memories?

I loved learning more from Iris about what mealtimes looked like in her German household. I was also kind of jealous to hear that she spent her childhood summers in Italy, such an exotic getaway compared to my own summers with my grandparents in the sleepy, southern Indian city of Trivandrum. While Iris equates food with survival, she did have quite a few favorite food memories.

"Cooking was a chore done in our house mostly by one of my brothers and me. My mother didn't cook much. However, mom did like to make Spaghetti Bolognese, so that was a frequent dinner option. During the summer we were frequently in Italy, so all in all, we typically ate German or Italian dishes.

In fact, I learned most of my cooking and got my favorite dishes from my grandmother who cooked northern German food including potatoes, herring, goulash, mett (minced raw pork), cauliflower, kohlrabi, and cabbage. One of my favorite meals is a red herring salad with German rolls. I love it! It reminds me of Germany and instantly transports me back there."

Can you share a favorite recipe of yours with me?

Iris is not a foodie, but she shared with me a recipe for Breaded Cauliflower, her favorite food in the universe that transports her virtually back to her native Germany. It is delicious and will certainly fill my heart with Iris memories every time I make it.

What advice would you give to your younger self?

Iris wished that she had more self-confidence to pursue the dreams and ideas she had when she was younger. But she acknowledges that if she had, maybe she wouldn't be where she is today.

> *"Try to live life to the fullest. You only live once. So, pursue your dreams, don't stand in your own way; pull out the expensive good china and glasses. What are you saving it for? Bad things will happen. It is simply not avoidable. But you can let those bad things bring you down or let them make you stronger. Don't be a victim, listen to yourself, and trust your instincts. Just be kind, be strong, be passionate about whatever you choose to do, and keep on learning and growing as a person."*

What do you want your legacy in the world to be?

I was also not one bit surprised when another super talented, accomplished woman stated she wanted her legacy to be around the humane person she was.

> *"Kind, caring, talented, and strong ...and yes, I will also be remembered as a perfectionist and stubborn. But why not?"*

MICHELE

S tate of mind: Bubbling insecurities as part of a high-performing, super talented team

I was hired into the start-up team that included a set of hand-picked employees and a super high performing team of consultants from a top-five consulting firm. I had a solid background in marketing, but my knowledge about the technical aspects of the internet was still in its infant stages. Every day, I heard a barrage of tech terms being thrown around; big process buzzwords were shared with abandon; voluminous PowerPoint decks boasted beautiful prose and visuals; and I felt more intimidated by the knowledge and talent that surrounded me.

I was learning, growing, and delivering so much each day, and wondered if it was possible to get to know some of my team members I was intimidated by a little bit better so I could learn and grow.

WHEN ILL HEALTH AND DEATH
BEGETS A FRIENDSHIP

Michele was a high-flying consultant from Accenture when I first met her. She was one of the many consultants assigned to work with us to launch a new brand of services that would take time and cost out of the very expensive, arduous task of bringing new medicines to the patients that needed them most. Ironically, it was illnesses where medicines could neither alleviate suffering nor prevent death to her loved ones that brought us closer as friends.

When I first met Michele, I was intimidated. She was smart, sassy, outspoken, and had that **NO NONSENSE**, arrogant "consultant" air about her - she had articulate answers to everything. I focused on putting my best foot forward with every interaction and friendship was the last thing on my mind.

· · ·

I picked up little bits and pieces about Michele during casual hallway banters, but it was her mother's cancer diagnosis that triggered a change between us. The person who I had seen as the hard-charging consultant was now the vulnerable daughter who wanted to do everything in her power to ensure her mother got better. She used her consulting experience to research doctors and cures, her negotiating prowess to cut through bureaucracy, and her program management skills to ensure that she met her work deliverables while being next to her mom at every stage of this life-altering journey. It was during this ordeal that Michele and I started exchanging messages; I sent her little snippets on cancer/ life/ positivity and she provided updates on how she and her mom were doing.

Michele may not know this, but her actions during this period taught me some valuable life lessons. I saw how she prioritized her mom over high profile career opportunities, how she talked about disease, illness, helplessness, and dying with grace and candor, how she stayed strong for others while her heart was breaking, and how she showed dignity to those who had wronged her family. And ultimately, when her mom passed, Michele paid the ultimate tribute to her – she bought her home and made it her own.

But I was not done learning from this amazing woman. In a cruel twist of fate, Michele's sister Cheryl, a young mom of three kids was also diagnosed with cancer. Cheryl lived nearly 1,500 miles away in Kansas and just like with her mother, Michele dove right in. She walked away from brilliant business opportunities, choosing the life of a consultant so that she could have the flexibility she needed to support Cheryl. Cheryl battled cancer for a few years. During this time, Michele made innumerable trips to Kansas, spending time with her nephews and niece while Cheryl got treated at the best cancer treatment centers. Sadly, Cheryl passed away, leaving behind a husband and three young kids. There is a saying that God sends his angels to protect you when the people you love pass, and Cheryl's little ones got the gift of Aunt Missy. Aunt Missy rearranged her entire life and put her own needs on the back-burner to ensure Cheryl's kids never lacked maternal love. A woman who never had kids of her own, but through her special, fun-loving, wacky, crazy personality enabled Cheryl's legacies to live a beautiful, loved up journey to adulthood.

When I was a kid growing up in India, there were some gross generalizations about life in America. *"People are self-centered; they don't sacrifice for others; they see family only on set occasions and this is all so different than life in India where love and sacrifices are offered without fanfare."* While my upbringing like those of many sure did teach me a lot about love, respect, and being there for family, it would not be an understatement to say that Michele was a living testament to these values. She taught me how to give unconditionally and to always do the right thing, without thinking about the consequences.

To me, Michele is an inspirer who unbeknownst to her has prepared me to deal with illness, death, uncertainty, and life choices with grace, dignity, and selflessness. We may not meet up often, but our intermittent text exchanges and our annual meet up at the same Starbucks in suburban New Jersey ensures that we keep abreast of each other's lives, sharing stories with ample doses of laughter.

A Q&A with Michele

.   .   .

What was your reaction to the tribute?

Michele, who works as a consultant to some of the largest companies in the US has carved a wonderful position for herself in work and life, working hard for months at a time and then taking time off to do the things she enjoys and cherishes. Michele had this to say about her tribute.

> *"My dear and loving friend — as usual your candor, love, and beauty shine through in your words. THANK YOU for this tribute."*

Michele's text and voice reactions to the tribute were so full of surprise and adoration, that it certainly made me smile.

What was your favorite memory of our time together?

Michele's memories of our friendship centered around feelings more than specific moments.

> *"My memory is fuzzy after my mother was diagnosed but I have a warm feeling in my heart & soul when I think of you because I know you were always kind & supportive in words and actions."*

How and where did you grow up?

Michele was born in Pawtucket, Rhode Island, in the same hospital and delivered by the same doctor as her mom and her sister Cheryl. Her parents were raised in New England — her mom in Rhode Island and her dad in Massachusetts. They met when they were both working at Texas Instruments and moved to New Jersey right after her dad got out of the army and went to college. This was also just around the time Michele attended kindergarten.

"As a child, I took my role of being a big sister seriously and after my parents divorced, my sister and I split the housework to help out. I focused on the inside and Cheryl focused on the outside (yard work, painting the house, etc.). My brother was too young, so his only job was clearing the table on Sunday (a responsibility we shared) and taking out the trash occasionally.

In hindsight, we all became a team and gravitated to our strengths. I think it was during this time that I realized if someone else had a skill for something, I didn't need to know what he or she knew; I just needed to know who to ask for help. So early childhood in a divorced parent's home taught me the importance of learning but stopped me from trying to become an expert at something that someone already had covered."

What was your personality like as a child?

I chuckled when Michele talked about being a fussy kid since it was one of the earliest traits I picked up about her; she liked things done a certain way.

"My mom would remind me that I whined a lot. I think I was a bit fussy just about everything; clothes itching, foods not to my liking, etc. I was taught that if you don't like something the way it is, you have to fix it or live with it, and not deal with it by whining.

While I outgrew some of this "complaining" trait as I got older, it is quite obvious when you get to know me that I still like things a certain way."

What did you want to be when you grew up?

I carry gratitude in my heart for some of my most influential teachers and those that helped my kids become the best versions of themselves. Becoming a teacher was a common childhood goal for many of my friends, Michele included.

"I have fleeting memories of wanting to be a teacher which might have been inspired by the Little House on the Prairie series. That was soon surpassed by my desire to be an engineer even though I did not know what that meant. It was subconsciously driven by a desire to show my Dad that I was stronger and better than him; he had gone to college to become an engineer but switched his major to business due to the curriculum challenges."

Michele became an engineer and has spent many years as a successful consultant transforming companies around the world.

What did mealtimes look like when you were growing up? Any favorite food memories?

I loved getting a glimpse into what Michele ate when she was growing up and was tickled when she shared images of recipe cards in her mom's and grandma's handwriting from decades ago. I found it interesting that her mom and grandma were organized with recipe cards and cookbooks, two things that were completely foreign objects in my childhood. Yummy healthy meals, rituals (like the ones Diane mentioned), and fussiness featured prominently in her mealtime stories.

"We always ate together and while I was growing up there was no soda or alternate beverages on the table – it was always a glass of milk for all of us including my mom.

My mom was a very good cook and I don't remember anything not tasting good. She had a habit of picking one recipe from her cookbooks for each meal and made copious notes on each one. Our rotation of meals included American, Italian, English dishes, and more with some of our favorites being macaroni and clams with red sauce, beef stroganoff with hamburger meat, and pork pie. Mom was quite creative with making up recipes including ones for a chilled tuna casserole (canned tuna, elbow macaroni, and French dressing) and a hamburg casserole (layers of shell macaroni, tomatoes, cheese, and marinated hamburger meat). Given she was a working mom, she also made as many lasagnas as she had pans and froze the extras for later.

We also had rituals. Friday night was normally hot dogs & beans and Sunday night was almost always steak with baked potatoes along with my grandmother's sour cream sauce. The cream sauce was a lifesaver that I smothered liberally on not just steak and potatoes, but also on vegetables to make them edible.

My fussiness came with me to the dinner table, and I often bailed on dishes simply because they did not look good to me. For years, I didn't eat my mom's Thanksgiving stuffing because it didn't meet my criteria of looking good and today it is one of my favorite foods.

Mealtimes during childhood are deeply ingrained in my memory and to this day, I have my mom's recipe box supplemented with some of my recipes. I like to pull out and make recipes written in her and my grandmother's handwriting. It brings such warmth to the soul and I would love to someday have the heart to recreate my mom's pork pie with her knack for making pie crust without her missing recipe."

To Michele, food is a word that comes to mind when she thinks of comfort, family, and her mom. And if there is one food that came up repeatedly for her cherished meals, it was lobsters.

"We were going to my grandparents' summer house in Matunuck, Rhode Island. It sounds fancier than saying a 2 bedroom itty bitty cottage on rented land. My mom stopped to pick up live lobsters as a surprise dinner for my grandparents and regaled us with a story from her childhood on how they would "borrow" lobsters from the traps and cook them over a bonfire in Matunuck. I think I realized for the first time that what we ate was alive once. My brother Paul couldn't handle this

information and proceeded to eat a hot dog instead of dinner and would not eat another lobster for about 15 years!

Lobsters became a celebration treat for us growing up and that tradition continues to this day for my brother and me. For his birthday dinner on Christmas eve, we combine lobsters with my mother's version of the Italian Feast of the Seven Fishes. My brother has added a fabulous signature touch to that tradition – shrimp wrapped in prosciutto & basil with a mustard sauce."

Can you share a favorite recipe of yours with me?

Michele went back to the good old sauce/veggie combo and shared her recipe for a cream sauce flavored with chives. This easy, yummy dish, will bring so many Michele stories to life.

What advice would you give to your younger self?

Michele's advice to her younger self centers on food and love.

"There is no downside to trying any food. My mom was never going to ask me to eat something that was bad for me ... so the best time to start is when you are a child.

Spend time with your loved ones while you can. As my mom told me years ago when my sister and I used to fight, you only have one sister – be good to one another. You won't get another one".

What do you want your legacy in the world to be?

When asked about what she wants her legacy to be, Michele's heart echoed sentiments similar to the ones mentioned by other friends.

"I've given this some thought, and I think simply – I want to be remembered by my people/universe as someone who loved with all my heart and was there when they needed support, joy, hugs, or extra love – through thick and through thin."

SUZANNE

S tate of mind: **Feeling on top of the world due to a big promotion and anxious about all the new disciplines to master**

It was a year into my new role at a large pharmaceutical company when I ended up landing a huge promotion. I went from leading one discipline to managing a large team and many areas that I knew little about. My team was a bit skeptical about my ability to support and manage them to success, and rightfully so. I was drinking from a fire hose, eager to learn as quickly as I could from my team and others while bringing my energetic, curious, out of the box thinking self to the role.

In a company where much knowledge was closely held and many relationships were deep rooted, coming in as an outsider was super hard. I fought to gain acceptance and looked for support in every conceivable corner.

THE MINNESOTA GIRL WHO
EXUDES PEP

PEP – According to the dictionary, the word can be a verb that means "add liveliness or vigor to someone or something". There could not be a more fitting word to describe my friend Suzanne.

Suzanne's energy found its way into my life when I inherited a new, complex area of business, health care economics and reimbursement. I knew very little about this space and the road ahead was unknown and scary. In stepped Suzanne, a consultant to our firm, her friendly voice assuring me that this was not rocket science and that she and her company would support me every step of the way. A consultant is paid to do just that, but this was not someone who was angling for the next piece of business. Here was a sensitive human being who understood that I needed help and joyfully built my confidence and skills.

. . .

Little did I know that a journey that started in this capacity would lead to a deep friendship, which would see us go from being acquaintances to friends whose conversations ranged from the frivolous (her perfect boots and hair) to the aspirational (watching polar bears in Manitoba) to the intense and painful (the agony and hope encountered when one battles metastatic cancer).

"Haaappppy Fridayyyyy! It's Suzaaaannnnne, I hope you are having a lovely day!"

"Hey Lakshmi, It's Suzaaannnnne.... I know this week is crazy for you and I wanted to reach out ...and let you know I'm thinking about you...."

"Hey Lakshmi, It's me.... I know it must be hard with your daughter moving so far away. I just wanted to check-in and see how you are doing."

In the decade that I have known Suzanne, I've received hundreds of these peppy messages. The kind of calls with no hidden agenda that exude positivity and envelope you with comfort at the end of a stressful day. I incorrectly assumed that Suzanne's Pollyanna personality must come from a life that was easy and beautiful; how wrong could I have been? Suzanne had been adopted as a baby, and as she encountered some health challenges, she struggled with having a blank slate for her medical history. Her son battled addiction for years and when he finally turned a corner, Suzanne was diagnosed with a rare, serious form of cancer. Her diagnosis went from bad to worse and yet nothing would breakdown her spirit, hope, or pep.

. . .

It was around this time that I lost my job in a downsizing effort at work. I went from feeling at the top of the world to the ultimate pariah battling feelings of rejection, shame, hopelessness; I was wallowing in self-pity when the pep girl reappeared. She connected me with people she knew, encouraged me, and boosted my confidence, all while she was fighting her own battles. As her combat with cancer grew more intense, she retired from work and found not just a beautiful, rich career evaporating overnight, but the disappearance of many friends and acquaintances as well. She would go on to theorize that it was simply because people were stumped on what to say and it was simpler to avoid such tough conversations.

Over the last couple of years, regular text exchanges have brought us even closer. We've chatted about the trips to far-flung places she is taking, the survivor conferences she is attending, the wigs she is wearing, the teeth that are falling out, the mind that is active but a body that is failing, the time with her grandchildren that leaves her beaming, and most of all her admiration, anger, frustration, and love for Jeff, her husband who is her rock star, supporting her each day through this rollercoaster ride called life.

Today, my friend Suzanne is a hero to me; a living, breathing legend who teaches me with every interaction to always chose life, love, and laughter no matter how bad things get. And when it gets really tough to maintain a friendship, that's when you embrace it and hold on even tighter.

A Q&A with Suzanne

What was your reaction to the tribute?

My beautiful friend Suzanne lives in Minneapolis with her husband and has three wonderful grown children and two beautiful grandsons who she refers to as the heart, joy, and light of her life. After years of working, Suzanne retired early during her battles with cancer. She is serving as a living example of "never giving up" by continuing her treatments and grabbing life by its horns, traveling as much as she can, and spoiling her family rotten. When my friend saw my first tribute, she had this to say.

> *"I'm in tears for your beautiful words and kindness. Your friendship means so much to me. Grateful, thankful, humbled are just a few words I can immediately think of. I am humbled and words are hard to come by. We have lived, loved, and fought for each other throughout our 10 years. You pop in via text on me seemingly when I need it the most, and my hope is that I was able to be a source of support for you when you needed it too. That's what friends are for – be they near or far – distance can't break a friendship."*

And I cried when Suzanne emailed this to me right after some pretty painful times with her health.

What was your favorite memory of our time together?

Suzanne's favorite memory twinned with mine when she recalled one of her favorite moments around us planning to travel to Manitoba together.

> *"Oh gosh – I still laugh about it to this day. We were having a great chat on the phone and talking about vacations and trips we'd like to take. I said, "I'd love to go to Churchill"; okay who else would know where Churchill was but you? You simply said, "Manitoba"? At that point, I just about fell off my chair and dropped the phone! We both learned how difficult a journey it was to get to Churchill. So, I propose we learn to speak Cree to each other before we go."*

How and where did you grow up?

Suzanne and I talked about a plethora of topics over the years, but I did not know that she was born in Los Angeles, California to a 14-year-old girl, and placed into adoption by the LA County Adoption Agency. She talked with much love and adoration about her parents.

"I was so fortunate to have been chosen by my mom and dad. I was the second of three kids and had a childhood that was filled with support with a stay at home mom, and a dad that worked as an engineer, in the aerospace industry. We lived in Southern California until I was a sophomore in high school when my dad was transferred to Colorado with Hughes Aircraft."

What was your personality like as a child?

Anyone who meets Suzanne will immediately notice a few details about her. She lives life full throttle; she is not fearful, and her energy is infectious. So, when Suzanne admitted to being a tomboy during her younger years, I was not the least bit surprised.

"When I was little, I was a tomboy, and to this day, I love to be outside whether it is summer, winter, spring, or fall. Hiking, camping, ice skating, snowshoeing, snowmobiling, dog sledding - basically, give me a challenge and I'll do my best to accomplish it.

During high school, I tried not to get typecast into a clique and was a cheerleader, a player on the soccer team, a member of the marching band, and also twirled a rifle.

Of course, I must add that I am someone who absolutely avoided conflict."

What did you want to be when you grew up?

As a kid, Suzanne loved to dance, and one of her fondest child-hood memories include doing the 2-step dance with her dad in the kitchen. So, dancing was the first career Suzanne wanted to take up when she grew up.

> *"I wanted to be a Radio City Rockette. Well, that changed as soon as I realized I would not grow taller than 5'2". I had a stubby leg kick that could rival that of any of those beautiful tall girls!*
>
> *When I could not become a Rockette, I decided that I was going to be a psychologist, and work with autistic children. Well, a Ph.D. in psychology, and my study habits, didn't mix, so off I went into commercial real estate, and one final change, that became my passion – healthcare.*"

Suzanne spent a number of years helping biopharmaceutical companies navigate the complex landscape of drug pricing and reimbursement before retiring to take better care of herself.

What did mealtimes look like when you were growing up? Any favorite food memories?

Suzanne grew up several continents removed from me. Yet, whenever she talked about money, her mom's cooking skills, and rarely going out to dinner, she sounded like she was recanting a page from my own life story.

> *"We always had family dinners. Since money was tight, we rarely went out to eat. My mom was a terrific cook, as was her mom. We'd have*

meatloaf, and fixings, spaghetti, and traditional meals, with a Scandinavian influence, which meant something wholesome and never spicy."

"When we had our kids, we continued the tradition and rarely went out to dinner. We always loved that time with the kids, whether I had to be a short-order cook, or not."

Both of Suzanne's parents were Swedish, so her favorite food memories hark back to those roots.

"Oh, there are so many food memories, but one stands out above the others. My parents were both Swedish, and so Swedish Potato Sausage was a standard during the holidays. While my younger brother and older sister liked Potato Sausage, helping make it wasn't their thing. I thought it was a great treat to learn the Swedish tradition and made it with my mom and dad. From getting the meat from the butcher, the casings for the sausage from a special place in Oklahoma, to grinding, filling the casing, and finally boiling it for freezing, or eating it immediately, I can still smell the wonderful aroma of the kitchen as everything was being prepared. How I miss that tradition."

Suzanne has been battling cancer for a number of years. So, it is not surprising that she now associates food with fortunate, sadness, and giving.

Can you share a favorite recipe of yours with me?

Suzanne shared the most gorgeous Baked German Pancake with Almonds recipe with me, which I have made a few times already. Not only is this a beautiful pancake to behold, but it is super easy and yummy.

What advice would you give to your younger self?

Asking her about the advice she would give to her younger self and her legacy was super emotional. Here's what Suzanne would tell her younger self.

"Take time to listen to the wind......it talks

Take time to listen to the silence......it speaks

Take time to listen to your heart......it knows

Listen...."

What do you want your legacy in the world to be?

When asked about the legacy she would like to leave behind, Suzanne texted me a very introspective message on this topic right after a doctor's appointment.

"Legacy is defined in the dictionary as 'something transmitted by or received from an ancestor or predecessor or from the past'. Given this definition, a legacy is not something that we have complete control over. After all, we cannot control how other people perceive us, we can only control our own actions. I have given a lot of thought to the end of my life, as my life was given an expiration date a couple of years ago.

Love......I hope I leave a legacy of love.

I hope that at the end of my days, friends, and those I've met along the way, when they hear my name, they associate it with love. Love for ourselves, love for one another, and love for this life. By living with our hearts, we can create heaven on earth. Love.

I hope that at the end of my days, my kids and my grandkids, feel like they had a mom, and grandmother, that loved them and showed how to love. One that helped them dream big and comforted them when they fell. Love.

I hope that at the end of my days, my husband feels I did a darned good job at being his wife. I hope to have shown him strength, dedication, and love to achieve the relationship that matters most to me in my life. His love."

SECTION 10
NUPURA

State of mind: Blissful and content, as a mom, wife, and professional

After the many twists and turns that my personal and professional life had taken, I found myself in a pretty rare state of both personal and professional contentment. I had two beautiful children who were growing up to be curious, sensitive, opinionated souls. I was super challenged at work but found tremendous joy in leading teams and mentoring extremely talented individuals. My husband and I were settled nicely into a comfortable existence in NJ surrounded by family (including my parents who had finally moved up) and friends, and it felt like a nice phase in life from every standpoint.

THE SASSY GO-GETTER WHO IS A WINNER ON ALL COUNTS

SASSY – Lively, bold, and full of spirit. That was my first impression of Nupura as we chatted away in Marathi at her front door with her dog Chiku intently watching us. I had stopped by to pick up my middle schooler who was chilling with Nupura's daughter. It did not seem like a first meeting as we talked for 15 minutes, crisscrossing an assortment of topics. Given our similar wavelengths, we promised to catch up more.

Soon after, Nupura had to go away on a business trip and since she did not have family in the area, asked if Sanjana could stay with us. I loved our first meeting and this simple act of trusting me with her daughter soon thereafter, made me want to know this no-nonsense woman a bit more. True to our promise, we started meeting up over meals, coffee, dessert, and sometimes just an impromptu glass of wine. With each interaction, I came to admire her just a little bit more. I nodded my head in disbelief at the adversities she had overcome, stared at her in awe for her guts, and burst into peals of laughter over some of her stories she shared.

Nupura was born and raised in India by parents who were both physicians. She had a lovely childhood and unlike the rest of her family who pursued medicine, she decided to study computer science. She met her husband, fell in love, got married young, and had a child soon after. At 23, this quiet peacemaker was on her way to her happily ever after. Her husband encouraged her to get her Masters, she got a good job, they moved to the US and lived here for a while before returning to India.

However, this fairy tale did not have a magical ending. Nupura began to tap into her reservoir of peacemaking skills to adjust to life with a crazy mother-in-law and an increasingly irate husband. While there was nothing that would change about her mother-in-law, she soon discovered that her husband's mood swings were a result of a full-fledged office romance. While Nupura had heard rumors, she never once gave credence to them. When her friend finally led her to the truth, heartbreak, anger, and deep sadness ensued. While many women within the traditional confines of Indian society might have worked it out and stayed put, the reel that played in her head led her to walk out. Sure, her husband had been supportive of her education and her career, but she knew she needed to be a model of self-sufficiency and self-respect to her daughter. She talked to her employer to secure a transfer and started a new life with Sanjana thousands of miles away with absolutely no support system in tow.

In a community where being stoic and not sharing a lot of emotion is lauded, Nupura told me her life story unadulterated, leaving me with a mixture of admiration for her candor and respect for her willingness to make tough choices. She continued to work hard at being an awesome mom, encouraging her budding aerospace engineer daughter while building a solid career and the financial stability to buy her own home.

Today, Sanjana is an aerospace engineer. Nupura, who started on her mental, emotional, and financial rehabilitation journey not too long ago is at the top of her game in all aspects of life. She takes trips with her daughter, does solo camping trips, brings joy to her parents in every conceivable way, and gives back by cooking for hundreds at an ashram in New York. Yes, Nupura is an outstanding cook and for a long time has dreamed of getting into the food business. But unlike me, she has acted on her dreams and launched her own catering business, piling up accolades and repeat business galore after just a few events.

Nupura is younger than me, but age is a meaningless measure in terms of who ends up inspiring you. Within a short span of under a decade, Nupura has shown me what one can do under the most heartbreaking of circumstances. She has lived what resilience means, given new meaning to the term 'hard work', demonstrated that being a role model means letting go and not living a life of bitterness, and most of all has shown me the power of honesty – how you don't have to pretend to be anyone, but the true version of yourself.

I cherish my intense conversations with Nupura, as much as I love our travel fueled discussions. I love our brief cups of coffee as much as our multi-hour dinner conversations. But most of all, I love that this spark called Nupura lights up my life with a form of joy that is priceless.

A Q&A with Nupura

What was your reaction to the tribute?

Nupura who lives in suburban New Jersey and works as a leader for a technology company had this to say when she read her tribute.

> *"Your words for me just brought tears to my eyes. I always try to live in the moment and never thought I had gone through so much in my life and achieved so many things. Thank you so much for writing this."*

Nupura's words moved me.

What was your favorite memory of our time together?

Like me, Nupura fondly recalled the many times we've shared.

> *"Lakshmi, I think each of our meetings has been memorable. We talk deeply about things; we laugh together; we become emotional together. Pata hi nahi chalta 3-4 hours kaise beet gaye (I don't know how 3-4 hours have passed).*
>
> *But I remember our first meeting to date. You came to pick up Sathya and you spoke Marathi with me. I was like, who is this lady who speaks Marathi, loves good food, loves to have fun, and loves traveling. Am I lucky or what? Those are the exact same things I love to do. No wonder we clicked immediately. It is fun to have you in my life, my friend."*

How and where did you grow up?

Nupura was born in Indore, Madhya Pradesh (in the central part of India), to two doctors and spent her early years in a joint family of 30 people in a huge home built by her great grandfather.

"Our family was a very forward-looking one, yet deeply rooted in its culture and traditions. In a country and an era where girls were not supported to study, our family produced high achieving women who were doctors, engineers, and professors. While today the notion of men doing chores is talked about extensively, the men in my family all cooked (better than the women), cleaned, and helped their wives.

My mom and dad pursued their graduate school education in Mumbai, so my grandparents had a huge influence on my life. My paternal grandfather was a humble man and an absolute gentleman. My paternal grandmother was a born leader and she was the reason my whole joint family stood together for years after my great grandfather passed away.

As a child, I saw my family work very hard to achieve great heights in both their careers and lives. I was especially influenced by the work ethic of an uncle who was an engineer (because being a doctor was so common in our family) and worked day and night to achieve his dreams."

What was your personality like as a child?

I talked about our meetups earlier; how they are fueled with conversations, laughter, and tears. It is hard to imagine Nupura as anything but vivacious. So, it came as a bit of a surprise to learn that she was a shy nerd outside the home.

"Growing up in a 30 person household, my personality and traits were molded from what I learned from my parents and the many people in my family who raised me when mom and dad were away at school. Some taught me to be grounded, others told me to work hard, and a group of them showed me how to have fun.

I was a very talkative, bubbly, fun-loving, laughing all the time, a naughty kid at home, but a very shy nerd who sat in a corner outside. In fact, this is a trait I carry to this day.

Given that I was raised in a joint family, everyone would know the instant I was upset and the whole family would keep asking me what happened, "why are you not talking or laughing or having fun"?

As a child, I loved playing ghar ghar (house) and making food and snacks. I loved my kitchen toys. Yet, I was an extremely picky eater and never ate anything. Most of the time, someone had to run behind me to get me to eat. Of course, that changed over time."

What did you want to be when you grew up?

When someone says they are clueless about their future, they usually get a weird look. Well, Nupura had no clue about what she wanted to be when she grew up and yet found her footing in life.

"I was such a happy-go-lucky child, that I lived in the moment. Now that I think about it, I really never thought about what I would become. I was unsure and just left it to life and God. All I knew was that I did not want to become a doctor as the thought of seeing people suffering just made me sad. Life really unfolded my career choices as I grew up."

Nupura became a successful computer engineer and in addition to being an amazing mom, leads mega technology transformation projects.

What did mealtimes look like when you were growing up? Any favorite food memories?

Having spent my childhood in India, I was very curious to see the similarities between our dinners. With both her parents working as physicians, meal prepping was a quicker ritual than for my stay at home mom.

"By the time my parents started practicing medicine, we were in a separate home with just the four of us. My sister and I looked forward to dinner time since that's when my parents would return from the clinic and start cooking a meal. We had a maid who helped with cutting vegetables and making rotis (fresh bread) and my mom would quickly make delicious vegetables. My sister and I arranged the mats, dishes, water, etc., formed a semicircle at the dining table or on the floor, and ate our simple meals while talking, sharing stories about our day, and laughing. Reminiscing about these moments brings the biggest smile to my face.

Besides everyday meals, each festival was like a bonanza celebrated with fun, laughter, and food — food which to Nupura is all about life, taste, flavor, joy, happiness, connections, love, togetherness, bonding, spicy, and chatpata (spicy, savory, sweet, salty all in one).

"Dinner on Diwali day in a joint family home was the best; for that matter any occasion/festivity at our large home was special. We would have a sit-down meal with our 30 family members and visitors, getting served the amazing festive food of Diwali by our cook, Daulat Ram. The food included a long list of Maharashtrian delicacies served with roti (bread), rice, koshimbeer (salad), and the dessert list included mouthwatering laddoos and shrikhand. Most of all, it is the experience of the whole family eating together that I will always cherish."

Can you share a favorite recipe of yours with me?

Dal is one of my favorite comfort foods and the fact that I could now make one more dal regularly (Nupura's dad's Onion Toor Dal) was just a happy coincidence.

What advice would you give to your younger self?

Women, in general, tend to be givers. As daughters, wives, moms, and employees, we give. So, Nupura's advice to her younger self touched a chord.

> *"I will tell younger Nupura to be as lively as she was but to only do 'just enough' for people so they don't take you for granted. It is human nature to just let someone who you can rely on handle things, but people forget that this person also needs caring. I just overdo things for people very close to me and learned this lesson the hard way. I would also tell the younger me to look after herself, which I only started doing later in life."*

What do you want your legacy in the world to be?

Nupura's wish for her legacy comes straight from a page in her life.

> *"I would want to be remembered as a very independent but family-oriented person who never cared about 'Log Kya Kahenge' (what will people think?). When people think of me, I want to be remembered as someone who derived her strength from her parents and God, forged her own path to becoming a successful professional, was the most rocking, awesome single parent to her daughter, formed an inseparable, dedicated relationship with her friends and ardent supporters, and most of all accomplished all this by staying true to her roots and traditions."*

PART IV
I SET OUT TO EXPRESS GRATITUDE; THE JOY GENERATED WAS PRICELESS

"People will forget what you said, people will forget what you did, but people will never forget how you made them feel." Maya Angelou

What were your reactions to the tributes and interviews with my friends? Could you see yourself in any of them? Could you picture any of these exchanges with your friends? Has a friend unexpectedly expressed gratitude to you? If so, how did that make you feel? If you have not received one, how would you feel if a bouquet of gratitude got delivered to you?

As you think about this, I'd like to share my personal experience from this journey. When I started this trip, I gave out few details about my intent or work. As I completed each friend's tribute, I reached out to her through a phone call and brief email, informing her that I had penned a tribute to acknowledge the impact she had on my life. I told her that I wanted to include her tribute in a book, hear her reactions to the acknowledgment, and also use this opportunity to learn just a bit more about her.

I honestly did not envision the deep joy a simple act of gratitude would spill forth. My friends were surprised; they were taken aback, and most of all each of them was genuinely touched by this gesture.

This unimagined, incredible, happiness generation cycle was a reminder to me to recognize more thoughtfully; a nudge to spend the time, to think about, and articulate what people truly mean to me. Did you get a chance to think about my earlier questions? How would you feel about giving or receiving a gratitude bouquet? I would guess the answer is, it would make you feel good. Do you have a friend you went to lunch with early on in your career? Or one that mentored you? Or one that got you through tough times? How about your family? Today is as perfect a day as any to express gratitude to them. A day to deliver an unexpected surprise, a moment to make someone feel that they matter. And in the process, just like me, you could enrich your own life with lots of smiles and maybe a few invaluable life lessons.

My forays in this gratitude journey have just begun. I thanked a small subsection of the individuals who made a difference in my life. There are so many more in my circle of family, friends, and acquaintances who I need to thank, recognize, and express gratitude to.

In a world where leaders are often seen as role models, what if each of us became leaders and role models for others on spreading gratitude? I somehow get the feeling that this simple act will leave both the giver and receiver with oodles of warm vibes. And where there are warm vibes, can happiness trail far behind?

PART V
PRECIOUS LIFE LESSONS
FROM A DIVERSE GROUP

Diverse is one of many words I could use to describe my special group of friends. They grew up in different places, practiced different religions, had different kinds of families and yet their memories were centered around basic universal human traits of love, fun, support, sharing, fear, food, and happiness. Isn't that an awesome message for the world today? Don't the headlines scream about how different we are? Our skin color, our religion, our political leanings, our attire, our food; every attribute dissected to show division. And yet, these eclectic group of women all found their way into my life and enveloped me with love and friendship. Did you see more similarities or differences in their stories?

Speaking of similarities, my conversations with my friends imparted some powerful, universal life lessons.

We are all part of the same tribe.

. . .

We run around as kids, learn little and big things from our parents, eat meals that invoke warmth in our hearts, develop personalities that we take to adulthood, have dreams of our grown-up versions, fight our insecurities, etc. Yet the privilege we are born into, the way we are raised, the neighborhoods we live in, the schools we attend, all lead us on different life journeys.

You can see our similarities in each of the stories shared and in a few simple examples.

Diane's parents in the US were telling her exactly what my parents were sharing with me 8,000 plus miles away in India – you can be anything you want to be as long as you work hard for it.

Anita reflected on our similarities when she spoke about friendship. *"Looking at it on the surface, what does a New York Italian have in common with a foreign-born Indian? Our kids got into trouble and we went from just being "moms" to individuals with lives, knowledge, and passion and developed a deep friendship."*

Hearing my friends' stories reminded me about an incident that happened many years ago when I was expecting my first child. A cab driver asked me what my dreams were for my kids. I said I wanted to raise them with values that I had imbibed growing up in India – be awesome at school, work hard to achieve your dreams, be confident in yourself, be compassionate and loving, and of course have fun. He was from Eastern Europe, a new immigrant himself, and very quietly made a powerful statement that has stayed with me ever since – *"Aren't these global values? Doesn't every parent raise their kids to be this way?"*

· · ·

We all battle insecurities.

The interviews with my friends reaffirmed how childhood feelings and experiences can be deep-rooted. Be it weight, money, or another issue, little comments heard at an early age have an indelible impact. Mona, Bess, and Sue talked about it. As a child, I was repeatedly reminded by my extended family that I did not match up in the looks department to many of my lovely cousins. In fact, a relative commented that my supposedly protruded teeth looked like the blades of a coconut scraper, a comment that led me to hide them whenever I smiled for a long time after. Like Bess, I too struggled to relate to my wealthier friends, feeling a deep complex about repeatedly visiting grandparents on vacation rather than taking off to exotic locales.

As I talked to my friends who I felt were so much more talented than me, I learned that they had their own insecurities, sometimes feeling they were the ones who were less talented/informed.

How much of our lives do we waste with these types of insecurities? How much time do we spend worrying that someone is more talented or knows more than we do? If the conversations with my friends are any indication of a broader universe of sentiments, shouldn't we try to let go of these fears and insecurities? This is so much easier to say than practice.

Being you is good enough.

· · ·

Each of my friends had advice for their younger selves. It centered around wishing they had been more content with who they were, that they pursued their dreams with passion, that they took a few more risks and, most of all, that they stayed true to themselves. That is a powerful set of messages from a super talented group of women. Personally, I had complexes about the way I looked; I wanted to study hotel management, which was unusual for South Indian families at the time. I did not love the sciences yet studied it because it was the smart thing to do. In hindsight, I wish I had the courage and confidence to stand up and say – "*I am me and this me is more than good enough.*"

You don't need to know what you will become when you grow up.

As a child and as a parent who has raised two kids, I found myself surrounded by people who seemed to have figured out at a young age what they wanted to be when they grew up. For those like me and others who did not have any clue, it was common to get a look that suggested that it was high time to figure it out. It was so gratifying to hear from my friends that I was not alone. Life is a beautiful journey that throws many opportunities along the way. While there is nothing wrong with knowing what you want to be, it is also perfectly okay to keep learning and growing and take detours along the way to get to where you are meant to be. Most of my friends did not become what they thought they would, yet each one landed in their own happy space.

Human values, not careers, create meaningful legacies.

. . .

My circle of talented, accomplished friends has achieved a ton in their professional lives, and yet when I asked them how they wanted the world to remember them, I did not hear about job titles, teams they led, products they launched, revenues they delivered, and more. Instead, I heard the following words and phrases – resilience, kind, caring, loving, supportive, loyal, brings happiness, made a difference, and more. So, while we live life in a rat race, let's not forget what makes us human, what makes us feel valued, what makes us tick – it is to love and be loved in return. PS. When I shared this finding with a family member, she wondered if men would respond similarly. Maybe that is a signal to do a similar project with men.

Learn from your grandmas while they are still around

Diane learned to cook from both sets of grandparents. Michele still uses recipe cards written by her grandmother and mother. Iris learned to cook from her grandmother. Each of these individuals shared very fond memories of learning about food, playing with it, and creating dishes with their grandmas. Just like friends, let's make it a point to learn from our moms and grandmas while we still have the chance. There is no better way to preserve their legacy than learning more about the food they feed us with love.

Food connects us and builds bridges

As a foodie, I absolutely had to understand my friends through the lens of food. Without exception, they recalled favorite childhood meals, talked about how food was a steppingstone into other cultures, and most of all how it was simply a metaphor for togetherness and happiness. Diane talked about a good meal being one where her grandfather turned down his hearing aid and basked in the company of his family; Mona talked about the meaning of togetherness at Thanksgiving; Nupura talked about her celebrations with 30 plus family members at the dinner table; I could go on about the exchanges that happened in my maternal grandparents' home with multiple generations involved in prepping, serving, and eating their meals in unison. In today's crazy world, it is important to remember that no matter who you are, where you come from, or who your friends are, a meal is a perfect way to connect and build bridges.

PART VI
A GIFT OF RECIPES

MARCIA'S QUICK TOFU HOISIN WITH BROCCOLI, RED PEPPER, AND WALNUTS

Ingredients:

For the sauce

- 1/3 cup Hoisin sauce
- 2 tbsp Chinese rice wine or dry sherry
- 1 tbsp toasted sesame oil
- 1 tbsp Tamari soy sauce

For the dish

- 2 tbsp vegetable oil
- 1 lb firm tofu, pressed dry into 2 x .5 inch pieces
- 6 cloves garlic, minced
- ½ tsp crushed red pepper flakes
- 1 red or orange pepper, cut into 3 x .5 inch strips
- 1 bunch broccoli, cut into florets (about 5 cups)
- ½ cup walnut halves
- 1/3 cup water

How to:

- Combine all the sauce ingredients in a small bowl and set aside.
- Heat the oil in a large wok or skillet till it is hot but not smoking.
- Add the tofu and stir fry till it is golden all over. Remove the tofu to a platter and reduce heat to medium-high.
- If there is no oil left in the pan, add a tsp or so. Add the garlic and red pepper flakes and cook for one minute.
- Stir in the red bell pepper, broccoli, and walnuts and toss to coat with the garlic. Add the water, toss and then cover the pan and cook for five minutes or until the vegetables are tender, yet crunchy.
- Stir in the tofu and the sauce mixture. Stir for a minute till the mixture is well coated and thickens and serve over hot rice.

SUE'S BANANA BREAD

Ingredients:

- Three small very ripe bananas mashed (about one cup)
- ¼ cup brewed coffee
- 1 tsp grated orange peel
- ½ cup sugar
- ¼ cup brown sugar
- ¼ cup unsweetened apple sauce
- 1 whole egg
- 1 cup whole wheat flour
- ¼ cup bread flower
- ¾ tsp baking soda
- ¼ tsp salt
- ¼ tsp baking powder
- ½ tsp ground allspice
- 1/3 cup chopped walnuts

How to:

- Preheat oven to 350 degrees Fahrenheit. Lightly coat a loaf pan with canola oil and dust with flour.

- In a small bowl, combine bananas, coffee, and orange peel. Mix well and set aside.
- In a medium bowl, mix sugar, brown sugar, and apple sauce. Add egg and mix well. Add to banana mixture and mix till smooth.
- In a small bowl, sift together the dry ingredients. Add to the banana mixture and mix till all the ingredients are just combined. Fold in the walnuts. Pour batter into prepared pan and bake for an hour or until a toothpick inserted in the center comes out clean.
- Remove from the oven and let cool on a rack for five minutes.
- Remove from pan and slice when cooled completely.

DIANE'S RICE CASSEROLE

Ingredients:

- 2 cups of rice (I usually use basmati)
- 1 cup toasted finely cut egg noodles (basically enough to sort of cover a baking sheet)
- 1/2 cup pine nuts
- 1 minced onion
- 4 cups warm vegetable stock

How to:

- In a decent size (~3 qt) covered casserole mix all the ingredients.
- Cover and bake at 350 degrees Fahrenheit for approximately 45 min. The dish will look moist, the noodles and nuts will rise to the top and brown a bit.
- Enjoy!

MONA'S HUMMUS

Ingredients:

- One small can garbanzo beans, drained
- 2 heaped tbsp sesame tahini
- 2 heaped tbsp whole milk plain yogurt
- 2 cloves garlic
- 1 tsp salt
- Juice of two lemons (Fresh lemons are the best, if you use it from a bottle, use 4-6 tbsp of lemon juice instead)

For Garnish:

- Extra virgin olive oil
- Paprika

How to:

- Rinse the garbanzo beans, drain them well and then pat them dry with a paper towel to get as much moisture out or your hummus will be runny.
- Blend all the ingredients in a food processor. Add additional salt, lemon juice, to taste.

- Before serving, top the hummus with paprika and good extra virgin olive oil.
- Serve with pita chips, tortilla chips, or pita bread.

BESS'S COLD TOFU WITH SCALLIONS

Ingredients:

- One block of soft tofu
- Soy sauce
- Sesame oil
- Salt
- Pepper
- Finely chopped garlic
- Finely chopped scallion

How to:

- Take one block of soft tofu and pat it dry.
- Cut the tofu in half and then slice into cubes leaving the tofu in its original block form. (Don't worry if the block falls apart a bit. The goal is not perfection, but rather to enjoy the flavors of this savory dish.)
- Sprinkle on wet ingredients first - soy sauce and sesame oil. Play with it. Taste as you go along to make sure the cubes are all coated.
- Then sprinkle on dry ingredients - salt, pepper, finely chopped garlic, finely chopped scallion.

ANITA'S PASTA E FAGIOLI

Ingredients:

- 2 tbsp olive oil
- One large onion, diced
- 2 cloves garlic, chopped finely
- One can cannellini beans
- 2 tbsp tomato sauce
- ½ tsp each of dried basil, oregano, and crushed black pepper (adjust to your taste)
- One cup pasta like mezzi rigatoni
- Salt
- Pepper
- Freshly grated parmesan for garnishing

How to:

- Heat the oil in a large pot to make the sauce.
- Throw in the diced onions and cook till transparent.
- Add the chopped garlic and cook that for a bit.
- Drain the liquid from the cannellini beans and add to the pot.
- Add the two tbsp of tomato sauce.

- Add the dried basil, oregano and crushed black pepper.
- Let this mix simmer on low heat.
- Cook the pasta separately in salted water and cook till al dente. Just before the pasta is cooked, add the beans to the sauce pot.
- Drain the pasta and save some of the water.
- Add the pasta to the sauce and add the saved water if it is too dry. But do not make it soupy.
- Serve hot topped with grated parmesan and crushed black pepper.

IRIS'S BREADED CAULIFLOWER

Ingredients:

- One whole cauliflower, rinsed and patted dry
- ½ or one stick of butter
- One cup seasoned bread crumbs

How to:

- Cook a whole cauliflower in a little bit of water till it is soft, but not mushy.
- Place the cooked cauliflower on a platter.
- Put the butter in a pan and let it melt. Add the seasoned bread crumbs to the melted butter and mix it together till the breadcrumbs absorb the butter.
- Put the bread crumb mixture on top of the cauliflower and voila it's done. It adds crunch and seasoning to the soft cauliflower.

MICHELE'S GRANDMA'S CREAM SAUCE

Ingredients:

- 1 cup sour cream
- 3 tbsp minced chive or onions
- 2 tbsp lemon juice
- 1.5 tsp salt
- 1/8 tsp pepper

How to:

- Mix all the ingredients well and serve with raw or cooked veggies.

SUZANNE'S BAKED GERMAN PANCAKES WITH ALMONDS

Ingredients:

For the pancakes

- 3 eggs
- ½ cup flour
- ½ tsp salt
- ½ cup milk
- 2 tbsp butter; melted
- 1-2 tbsp butter; softened

For the almond topping

- ¼ - ½ cup sliced almonds
- 1 tbsp butter; melted
- Pinch of sugar

How to:

- With a wire whisk, beat eggs until blended. Sift flour, measure, and sift again with salt. Slowly add flour mixture to beaten eggs, beating constantly, until smooth.

- Next, add milk (1/4 cup at a time) beating slightly after each addition. Gently beat in 2 tbsp melted butter.
- With 2 tbsp of softened butter, butter bottom/sides of a 9, or 10" cast-iron skillet.
- Pour batter into a cast-iron skillet. Bake at 450 degrees Fahrenheit for 15 minutes, quickly sprinkle with almonds and sugar and drizzle melted butter. Let bake for another 5 minutes.

NUPURA'S ONION TOOR DAL

Ingredients:

- ½ cup toor dal
- Salt to taste
- ½ tsp turmeric
- 1-2 green chilies finely chopped
- 2 tsp oil
- 1 onion finely chopped
- ¼ tsp asafetida
- 1 tsp cumin seeds
- 1 tsp red chili powder
- 1 tsp coriander powder
- 1 tsp garam masala
- 3 tbsp finely chopped cilantro

How to:

- Cook the toor dal in a pressure cooker with the salt, turmeric, and green chilies till done, without the dal getting mushy. In the Instant Pot, this will take 15 minutes at the high-pressure setting, with a manual pressure release.

- When the dal is cooked, heat the oil in a pan. When the oil is hot, add the chopped onion, asafetida, and cumin seeds. Sauté till the onions turn dark golden brown, but don't get burnt.
- Now add the red chili powder, coriander powder, and garam masala and cook for 30 seconds.
- Add the cooked toor dal and the cilantro to the onion spice mixture, stir well, and take off the stove.
- Eat the dal hot with rice or roti.

THANK YOU TO MY SUPPORT SYSTEM

If I had to say thank you, it would have to be to an entire universe of family, friends, colleagues, and strangers who have each contributed to making me the person I am today. I am the product of my life experiences. But, in the spirit of being more specific, I would have to thank a few people for the specific gifts they have imparted to me.

I was fortunate to have all four of my grandparents alive until I reached the age of 21 and their brilliance, humility, emphasis on education, and bringing family together through good food are lessons that have been a guiding compass. My parents did not have a lot of money, but without their unending list of sacrifices, contributions, and support, I wouldn't have gotten where I am today. I met my husband when I was 17 and since that day, he is the person who has always had my back and has more faith in me and my abilities than I ever could. My life would be incomplete without the most precious gift from my two girls – the gift of motherhood. I started as a parent but have learned so many precious lessons from them. In fact, the older one helped edit this book, and the younger one sketched my friends' faces that went on the cover. My sister-in-law, my brother, and their two kids have lived in the same town as me for the past 24 years and the support, love, joy, and inspiration they have provided has been endless. A special thank you to my close-knit family, especially my cousins and my four nieces who have given me much inspiration and happiness over the years.

While I have highlighted ten women in this journey, there are so many others that have provided incredible inspiration, support, and joy over the years. I'd like to give a shout out to a few of them. Dipti Sanghani - we met in school in India, moved to the US around the same time, and traveled so many highs and lows together; Sushama Gunjal - who has been a rock through my entire existence in the US, but is too private to participate in a public forum; Cathy Barnett - who unknowingly taught me to be a super fun mom and to plan the most meaningful celebrations; Andrea Kraft - who mentored me through my Marriot years; Susan Thronson – who gave me the launchpad for a global career; Cindy Van Dijk – who has been an amazing model of resiliency and joy over a multitude of moves and adversities; Suzanne D'Amico-Sharp – who was the first to acknowledge the arrival of my second baby and has been a cheerleader through this book writing journey; Jayasree Natarajan - whose infectious laughter got me through some crazy kid rearing years; Greta Brown - for being the most gracious and supportive neighbor friend; Giordana Marioni – who was there for me through some tough personal and professional times with ample amounts of espresso and prosecco; Maria Cristina Cedrini and Claudia Leoni – for bringing their entire sense of Italian well-being into my life; Debbie Stark - For bringing levity to the experience of raising kids; Kristina Pedlar – who has filled my life with much laughter, eye ball rolling, and cakes; Dawn Van Wagenen – who taught me about areas I knew little about, including overcoming my fear of animals; Evanne Cuzzocrea – who has been a quiet, unwavering source of inspiration with her love story with Pete and her dedicated care of her mom; Shabnam Kazmi – our kids started preschool together, but we have bonded more recently on topics ranging from dementia to how south Asian women are struggling to break through the glass ceiling. While I have named a few of the women, I would be remiss if I did not mention my kids' friends; these young men and women, many of whom spent countless hours in our home have provided me so much inspiration, joy, and learning through their journeys.

And to each and every male boss/mentor/friend who enabled me in my journey, I would not be here today without you.

This book would have been a pipe dream without the help of my friends who jumped on the bandwagon with me and trusted me with their stories. Thank you for the love, support, and joy you have given me over the years. A big thank you to Mr. Kessler, my children's middle school English teacher. I learned to become a better writer from reading his feedback to my kids. And when I completed the first draft of this book, he generously agreed to read it and provided me with invaluable feedback. Thank you to Chuck Hopper, a former colleague and present friend, who connected me to a published author, Corrina Lawson. Corrina patiently gave me a lot of tips on how to survive the writing journey. A quick thanks to Leena Mankad Saini, who encouraged me to step up to rejection and continue my journey fearlessly.

And a heartfelt thank you to each and every one of you who have read this. If this book brings forth one more expression of gratitude from each reader, it would be another little turn in moving the happiness wheel forward.

ABOUT THE AUTHOR

Lakshmi Sundar is an incredibly curious daughter, wife, mother, citizen of the world who has an insatiable appetite for new experiences. A strategist, marketer, and change agent by profession, a traveler and adventurer by passion, a storyteller in her Zen state, and most of all someone who is at her blissful best around the topic of food! Lakshmi's motto in life is to jump into situations she knows little about and navigate her way to incredible experiences, beautiful relationships, and positive outcomes.

This is Lakshmi's first book.

 twitter.com/aglobalaffair
 instagram.com/aglobalaffair

Made in the USA
Monee, IL
02 April 2024